DAPHNE SELFE

The Way We Wore

A Life in Clothes

MACMILLAN

First published 2015 by Macmillan
an imprint of Pan Macmillan
20 New Wharf Road, London N1 9RR
Associated companies throughout the world
www.panmacmillan.com

ISBN 978-1-4472-9191-6

1 3 5 7 9 8 6 4 2

A CIP catalogue record for this book is available from the British Library.

Illustrations by Heather Gatley

Printed and bound by CPI Group (UK) Ltd, Croydon, CR0 4YY

Visit www.panmacmillan.com to read more about all our books
and to buy them. You will also find features, author interviews and
news of any author events, and you can sign up for e-newsletters
so that you're always first to hear about our new releases.

For my grandchildren

Robin, Grace, Alec & Jack

Contents

Introduction

Nick Knight, one of the world's leading photographers, is doing a shoot for Vogue. *The model is posing in a scarlet Hussein Chalayan dress so figure-hugging that she can't wear any underwear. The famous hairstylist Sam McKnight has done her hair in a Grecian style and she has bare feet. There's nothing unusual about this scene – except that the model is me and I am seventy years old.*

This was 1998. Suddenly as an older model I was in fashion – literally – and I was enjoying every minute of it. The stylist and I couldn't stop giggling as we tried out different ways to wear my very clingy jersey dress. After several false starts we got there without disrupting my hairdo, but the knickers had to go, as anything under this particular outfit showed an unwelcome line.

It was all very unexpected. If you had asked me twelve months earlier what I thought I would be doing in a year's time, the very last thing I would have said was, 'modelling for *Vogue*'. What is so strange is that I was 'discovered' once, at twenty-one, when I was chosen for the cover of *Reading Review* magazine, a job that led to several successful years as a model in 1950s London. Then I was 'discovered' again at seventy, when I was enlisted to 'walk' for the designers Red or Dead during London Fashion Week and subsequently asked to model for *Vogue*. Having two bites of the cherry in very different eras has been quite fascinating, as modelling and everything else had changed so much in fifty years.

Mine is not a rags-to-riches story, nor have I had to overcome incredible odds. I have just been lucky and able to appreciate the amazing chances and coincidences that have come my way. It has been an ordinary life in which extraordinary things have happened, and it has encompassed nearly a century of fashion along the way, especially as I have always been interested in clothes. So this is the story of my life and style, from the day my parents met over a single 'Gibson' shoe to my latest campaign for a major clothing company, taking in Dior's New Look, Courrèges's shift dresses and 1970s flares and bell-bottoms – to name but a few – in the process.

Seventeen years after that *Vogue* shoot, now aged eighty-seven, I am still busy modelling – and still amazed.

ONE

One White Shoe

It wasn't a glass slipper – it was a white canvas shoe with a single strap, a narrow toe and a low, curved Louis heel, the type of shoe that every stylish young woman was wearing in the summer of 1915. Yet it had just as much symbolic significance in my family story as Cinderella's lost slipper – because, without it, my parents might never have met.

The shoe was known as the 'Gibson', a classic style that epitomized the footwear of the glamorous Gibson Girl illustrations in the American magazine *Harper's Weekly* – a very clever piece of promotion! One afternoon, it fell off a hotel balcony in Lowestoft, Suffolk, and landed on the next floor down, where it was discovered by a schoolteacher in his mid thirties who probably wouldn't have been able to distinguish it from a Mary Jane or an Oxford.

A quiet, unassuming sort of chap, Francis Selfe was in Lowestoft enjoying the famous beaches, piers and sunrises with his brother and sister-in-law, just back from India, and their six-year-old son John. Lowestoft was *the* place to go in those days. It had been fashionable since the 1760s, when the first bathing machine was introduced, and in the first half of the twentieth century it competed for popularity with East Anglia's other hotspot, Cromer.

Francis rescued the shoe from his balcony and set off upstairs, where he knocked on the door of the rooms above his.

'I was wondering if this belonged to anyone here?' he asked shyly.

Whose foot would fit the dainty shoe? Among the guests on the next floor up were several members of a large family called the Garraways and, as luck would have it, the youngest of them stepped forward to claim it. She was a radiant twenty-two-year-old named Irene, affectionately known as 'Babie' – a real Irish beauty, with auburn hair, deep-set blue eyes and high cheekbones. Just a few minutes earlier, she had cleaned her shoes and put them out on the balcony in the sun to dry, only for one of them to topple off the side.

'Yes, it's mine,' she said with an apologetic smile. 'I'm sorry to cause you the trouble of coming up here.'

'Not at all,' he murmured, trying not to stare. 'It's no trouble.'

By the time my father got around to introducing himself, he was already in love, but it wasn't going to be Happy Ever After quite yet. The two families struck up a friendship and spent pleasant hours promenading together in the sunshine – and at some point he proposed to my mother. But she turned him down.

Decades later, I could tell by the way they recounted their first meeting that there had been an immediate spark between them, but Mummy was already inundated with suitors. Her admirers included Marconi, the inventor of the radio, and she had been painted by the fashionable portrait painter Gerard Leigh Hunt. Considered a great beauty, feted by everyone, she was in a position to be selective – and perhaps my father was a little old for her. It was, after all, a gap of fifteen years. She didn't think it a good idea to marry an older man. Still, they stayed in touch when the holiday ended.

Daddy couldn't go into the war because of his poor eyesight, so became a Civil Defence Warden and carried on his teaching career. He wrote regularly to my mother during the war years. People wrote a lot of letters in those days. I wouldn't think she bothered to reply – or not very often, if at all. Their paths may even have crossed at the occasional salon or soirée, where my mother would sing and play piano. She was a superb musician and singer. Either way, he would have been painfully aware that over the next few years she was busy getting engaged to other people.

Her first fiancé was Harry Satterford. Then she was engaged to Tom Cade. Both men were cruelly killed in the war. I have no idea how deeply she was affected by their deaths, partly because more than two decades had passed and another war was upon us by the time I got to hear about it. Even then, I wasn't told much – and it wouldn't have done for me to ask. It was off-limits somehow. People didn't talk about their feelings. So I don't know if her heart was broken once, or twice, or if she simply got caught up in a whirlwind of romantic farewells on station platforms, barely knowing the men she promised to marry when they got back from the Front. Engagement was a very loose term in those days. You had to practically get engaged to somebody before you went out with them. The social code was different – it was a different world altogether with so many men being killed, something that all the young British women of the time had to contend with. Many of my aunts and their friends remained spinsters for the reason that most of the eligible men went away and very few returned.

There were other changes to adjust to. Women were required to work during the war years, and Mummy got a coveted position at the Bank of England by virtue of her beautiful handwriting. This was a complete turn-around, as my grandmother hadn't allowed her to get a job when she left school. The Bank was very security-minded and she was locked in a cage for hours on end while she laboured away writing up the ledgers, but at least she could look forward to an amazing seven-course dinner at the end of the day. Everyone else was starving but the bank people had a banquet every evening.

Women's fashions were changing too. Big things were happening in Paris, where everything was becoming Modern. The influential designer Paul Poiret had almost single-handedly put an end to the wearing of Victorian corsets with his simple, loose-fitting designs and love of layering. Poiret's silk kimono coats were all the rage; Coco Chanel's chemise dresses encouraged a more natural line; Jeanne Lanvin designed summer shift dresses that freed women's bodies from the starchy restrictions that had come before; and the modern bra was invented (hooray!). Stiff materials and whalebone made way for flowing silk, satin, cotton and wool. Hemlines rose to midway up the calf, waistlines loosened and swimsuits crept above the knee – although most women still wore stockings underneath them, in the sea as well as on the beach!

My mother loved the new silhouettes, of course. She was a stylish girl about town then and continued to be fashion conscious throughout her life. She always dressed well – and made sure that I did too – even in her later years. I enjoyed dressing up my girls to please her, as she liked them to be in fashion. 'What are you wearing today? What have Claire and Rose got on?' she'd ask.

So, of course, she went in for the craze for fuller, shorter skirts that dominated the magazines of 1915 and

1916, known as 'war crinolines', which at last enabled women to be people of action, rather than taking dainty little steps everywhere they went. They caused a lot of controversy, with people condemning them for the excessive material they required in times of shortage, or denouncing the improper skirt lengths. But the fashion writers claimed they were 'patriotic' because seeing women's ankles lifted the spirits of soldiers on leave, which I'm absolutely sure it did.

Fashion sobered up the following year and women wore more muted outfits, in keeping with the sombre mood of the country. Everywhere you looked, people were mourning sons, brothers and husbands. The soft pre-war pastels and bold colours favoured during the first optimistic years of the war were now rarely seen, and military influences crept into the latest jacket, shoe and coat designs, as they did again during the Second World War.

Mummy got engaged for a third time, to Bert Windsor, who survived the war, but the relationship faltered – although they stayed in touch and I remember meeting him and liking him very much, years later when I was married. Meanwhile, my father remained patiently loyal. He got the girl in the end, but she did make him wait!

Although he wasn't her first choice, it strikes me that my mother was actually well suited to life with an older man. Her father had died suddenly at the age of forty-two, when she was only nine, and I think Daddy filled the gap left by that appalling loss. He was the doting, paternal type and he adored her. Maybe she'd been looking for a father figure all along.

She must have longed for security, because her family had been through precarious times after her father's death. It was a real struggle for my grandmother Emily Garraway, who was left a widow with five children. No health service, no welfare, all those children and no husband! How difficult it must have been, but she got through it. Her brother, Fred, was apparently a great help. I never knew him but he sounded a wonderful and supportive man.

My grandmother Emily – perhaps fortunately, in the circumstances – was no stranger to turbulence and up-heaval. Her family had fled the Irish famine in the 1850s and headed for New York, where she was born in 1859. But within a decade they migrated again, this time to Stroud Green in North London, where she married my grandfather when she was twenty-one. Tragically, her second child, Dora, died after being tipped out of a pram by a careless nursemaid, which must have been the most awful blow. But I don't think people made as much out of personal tragedy as they would now. They lacked knowledge and didn't talk about such things. Psycho-analysis was unheard of, there was no counselling, no outside help. Your friends and family helped you through your troubles and you just had to get on with it. Some people managed and others didn't do so well. Everything depended on how strong you were within yourself – and Grandmother Emily was strong.

My mother was born in 1893, the sixth and final child: Irene, the 'Babie'. A gifted musician, she was strong and positive, like her mother, and learned early on how to make the best of things. The only time life got her down – that I know of – was when she took her London Royal Academy of Music (LRAM) exam and failed by only one mark. This brought on a nervous breakdown, or so she said, although there was never any sign of a delicate mental state that I ever saw. Anyway, it can't have been that bad, because she continued with her music, practising at the piano for four hours a day and playing all over London, at Masonic dinners and concerts at prestigious venues like Wigmore Hall. I still have some of the programmes, because I'm a terrible hoarder.

Mummy and her older sister Gertie learned singing with a teacher named Smythe, who was a friend of the great Italian operatic singer Enrico Caruso. Mummy said that he looked like Caruso and lived in a garret up a little back alley, which makes him sound rather romantic. He told her that she had a natural voice with a velvet quality, and after he had taught her all the rudiments of singing, she began to sing at the 4 p.m. *thés dansants* at Bentalls department store in Kingston. Leonard Bentall was a good family friend. During the war she sang at St Martin-in-the-Fields, the Skinners' Hall and Fishmongers' Hall.

The Garraways were a sociable family and held musical evenings every second Tuesday in the month. People arrived with sheaves of music or poetry books and everyone wore their best clothes: short party dresses, fans with feathers and hats from Bourne & Hollingsworth on the corner of Oxford Street, which had streamers down the back, cost 4 shillings and 11 pence and were decorated with velvet and cherries. The sideboard and wagonette were crammed with food – sandwiches and sausage rolls, jellies and coffee – all home-made.

Grandmother Emily used to recite. She was a striking woman with a lot of hair and everybody said she ought to have been an actress because she was very good at delivering a monologue with background music and actions. As for the rest of the family, Gertie did a sketch, Gertie's husband, Otto, played the piano and my mother sang songs like, 'Where My Caravan Has Rested', 'Two Eyes of Grey' and 'Listen to the Watermill'.

Who knows what Mummy was expecting from life before the Great War came along? Something more dazzling than marriage to an older, bespectacled teacher, I'll be bound. But the 1914–1918 war dashed everybody's hopes and expectations, and she was fortunate to be able to turn to my father when it ended.

Things were different after the war and marrying an older man wasn't unusual because so many of the young men had died. At last she made up her mind to accept his proposal and became Mrs Francis Selfe on 9 August 1919. At the wedding, she wore a flowing two-tiered embroidered lace dress, loosely structured, with a drop waist, in a style that was most definitely looking ahead to the fashions of the 1920s. The material can't have been easy to come by, what with all the post-war shortages, but she managed it somehow. She was also draped in a veil that dated back to 1862, an exquisite piece of delicate Brussels lace embroidered with intricate flower patterns. It belonged to my father's aunt, Lady Carr-Selfe, who had worn it at her wedding more than fifty years earlier.

As for Daddy, he was in morning dress, of course, which might have been rather boring in comparison to his beautiful bride's cascading lace, were it not for his white carnation buttonhole, his elegant Beau Brummel walking cane and the dashing pale grey spats covering his shoes. People really knew how to dress up for weddings in those days.

Wonderfully, Francis and Irene went on to spend forty years happily married until he died at the ripe old age of eighty-one, in 1960. They lived through insecure times and had a couple of dramatic economic crashes after I came along, but nothing seemed to dent their happiness.

She was the boss in the marriage. He was the perfect gentle-man. I never once saw them have a row.

It's sweet that he waited so long for her. Maybe he was chastened by the fact that his banker father, John Selfe, had been through a divorce. John's first marriage to Clara Maberly produced no children, whereas his second, to Laura Jane Aylwin, produced eight! The whys and wherefores were never explained – one can only specu-late, especially as Clara also remarried – but I wonder if John advised his son on the powers of attraction and the importance of making sure one married someone with whom one was completely in love. For my father, that person was Mummy, and only Mummy.

His family were originally from King's Lynn in East Anglia, but by the time he met my mother they were living in Sydenham in South London. He was born in 1878, which seems so very long ago now! He went to school at Dulwich College followed by three years at Magdalene College, Cambridge, where he gained a first-class honours degree and a classical tripos. He could have gone on to study for his Masters, but he wanted to take orders and be ordained into the Christian Ministry. In the end, he did neither, as it was too expensive to continue his studies – and so he decided to become a schoolteacher.

One of his first jobs was coaching undergraduates for the Army and Navy entrance exams. He taught at Kent

House and later at Eastbourne College where, being a keen golfer, he started the golf club. He was a brilliant academic but also an excellent sportsman. He played everything, from squash and tennis to cricket, and rowed for his college.

A gifted teacher, he could coach even the dullest boy to pass. 'Oh, sir,' they would say, 'you make it sound so easy!'

He used to write the school plays and act in them – much to the boys' amusement. He also loved music and could sing and play all the Gilbert and Sullivan operas, note for note, word for word. Long after they were married, he and my mother sang together in the Reading Operatic Society and, of course, that included Gilbert and Sullivan.

Their first move, in the autumn of 1919, was to Cobham in Surrey. Daddy had previously bought a house in Kent for £26 but Mummy refused to live there. It was too tiny and too far from her family and so they had one built and named it Thurlstone, after a village in Devon they had visited on their honeymoon. The house was a short walk from Sandroyd, the boys' prep school where Daddy taught many a boy who went on to great things, including the politician Randolph Churchill and the playwrights Terence Rattigan and N. C. Hunter.

My mother looked back on the years before I was born as a halcyon time. 'They were happy and carefree days with not a worry in the world,' she used to say, adding, 'We had lovely coal fires everywhere.'

My father earned £500 a year, which with good, careful management enabled them to run a Bullnose Morris Oxford car and employ several servants. The nanny was a pound a week; Edith, the young cook, was paid £1 5 shillings a week; and Cleaver, our gardener, £1 10 shillings. Cleaver wore an overall and a baize apron. He cleaned our shoes, chopped the wood, brought in all the coal and logs, cleaned the 'Cook's Joy' – which was the stove – and the steps and windows. The rest of the day he worked in the garden with my father, and helped make the tennis court the best in Cobham. Along with his salary, he got all his lovely veggies and fruit free.

They had goats for a short while – a gift from some friends – but these turned out to be a disaster, as they kept escaping and eating the roses. Daddy took great pride in his roses and the goats had definitely overstepped the mark, so they ended up in a pot on the 'Cook's Joy'. Goat stew, delicious!

Whenever Mummy gave a dinner party, although she never invited more than six people, she employed at least two extra staff to help out: a cook in uniform with cap and streamers, and what she called 'a first-class parlourmaid'. On the morning of the dinner, she would cycle to Cobham to tell the cook which food and wines were required. Then the cook and parlourmaid would arrive on their bikes at three o'clock to prepare a seven-course dinner by seven thirty.

'I had no fault to find and didn't have to tell them anything,' she recounted years later. 'I wrote it all down first and it was served on the stroke of seven thirty. They worked together and did all the washing-up – and nothing was out of order when I went out to look at the kitchen and pantry afterwards. Now I look back on it, it really was marvellous. Believe it or not, the cost was 10 shillings and 6 pence for the cook for the evening and 7 shillings and 6 pence for the parlourmaid. Edith, our little maid, was sent upstairs to help with me until the two women went off on bikes at twelve o'clock in the dark, with only lanterns, and not a grumble from anyone.'

Among their neighbours were some very rich and well-known people, including Sir Ernest Shackleton, who lived in great style in a huge house nearby – when he wasn't away battling ice and snow in the Antarctic, which was, admittedly, most of the time. They went to dinner at the Shackletons' several times before he died in early 1922, and afterwards too, I think.

Everyone had a tennis court and there were lots of tennis parties in the summer. Daddy was always the star turn. No one could beat him. About twice a week, they'd go to someone's house for dinner wearing full evening dress and patent shoes. 'We nearly always stayed till twelve o'clock and when we left, we walked back, as it was so near,' Mummy recalled. 'Our lovely black pussy-cat, George, would always be there to meet us. He'd wait in the tree opposite until we came out and then run on in front of us, leading the way back home.'

Just opposite Thurlstone lived Gerard Leigh Hunt – whom my mother described as a dapper little man, not a bit like an artist – and his wife. Mummy already knew Leigh Hunt from the time he had painted her at his studio in London, when she was nineteen. The portrait hangs above my bed, as it has done for many years, and I absolutely love it. The day of the sitting was particularly windy and she pedalled to his studio on her bicycle. By the time she arrived, the feather on the hat she was wearing had been bent right down, and that's how he painted her – bent feather and all. It makes for a very eye-catching composition.

Other local friends were Sir Malcolm and Lady MacAlpine. Two of their sons went to Sandroyd and Daddy coached one of them to pass his Common Entrance. The MacAlpine mansion, Fairfield, was only ten minutes' walk away from Thurlstone. It was a beautiful house, filled with flowers, and they had a butler and a large staff of maids. There was also a footman who, much to my mother's amusement, answered the front door and then walked backwards until he got to the drawing-room door, at which point he announced the guests.

Mummy once wrote to me that Lady MacAlpine called one afternoon at Thurlstone soon after I was born, 'bringing lots of fruit and flowers from their gardens, and a sweet little pink coat that she had made for you, and stayed to tea on a gorgeous day. She also came to show me her new little car, in green. Her new toy, only just out, it was hers alone for little journeys. They also had a magnificent Rolls-Royce in black, with chauffeur.' She was a treasured friend.

Lady MacAlpine didn't seem to mind in the least that Sir Malcolm had taken a shine to my mother and kept taking her everywhere. Mummy clearly saw nothing wrong in it either, recalling a dinner where, 'Malcolm was an absolute poppet. He was telling us all about the building of the Dorchester in Park Lane and I went up to see it with him before it was finished. He said, "You must come up for the opening." I was thrilled. I never saw anything so perfect.'

Sir Malcolm co-owned the Dorchester and the opening was quite an event. After a ceremony officiated by Lady Violet Astor, a gala luncheon was held for a list of guests that included the Foreign Secretary Sir John Simon, the BBC's Lord Reith, and Margot Asquith, Countess of Oxford. Mummy had a marvellous time and was entranced by the restaurant with its pink lighting and mirrors, which made her look more beautiful than she already was!

My father didn't mind her going out with Sir Malcolm. He doted on her and would have gone along with anything that she did. She had him – and a lot of men – wrapped round her little finger. The wildly popular dance-band leader Geraldo was another fan. I'm sure she didn't have affairs, she just had a lot of friends, like everyone else. I've always had admirers, too – although these days they are mostly gay, which is great. I've met a lot of wolves in my time and I can't stand them.

My parents had been married for nine years before I arrived, so I must have come as quite a surprise. Maybe they just put it off, or maybe they didn't! I've no idea as people didn't talk about it. They still don't talk about it, do they? A bit more than we used to, perhaps. Anyway, I'm not sure if she longed for a child all those years. I'm not a baby person myself, and I don't think she was, either. I love children – and I love them now they're all grown up. I think I'm better with them now than I was.

There are no photographs of Mummy when she was expecting me, as I don't suppose it was the done thing to capture a woman on camera during a pregnancy. There may have been a bit of vanity involved, too. Having adopted the flapper look from the start of the 1920s, she found herself constantly irritated by her big bosom, which didn't fit the boyish silhouette of the flapper girl at all. All these years she had worn a broad, home-made elastic band to flatten her chest, but pregnancy, with its inevitable expansion and tenderness, might well have consigned it to the dustbin.

She probably wore a maternity corset, with elastic panels and adjustable lacing. It sounds worse than it was – and was nothing like the horrible contraptions that the Victorians wore to squash and conceal their pregnancies. In the late 1920s, a maternity corset was advertised as being a 'healthy' option that supported a growing bump, although it probably had a minimizing effect as well. I'm pretty sure that she would have owned one, because in later life she always wore a corselette – a longline undergarment that simultaneously acted as a bra and a girdle. These had a bit of give and weren't boned like the corsets of old, but were full-length and had suspenders attached. Either way, she was lucky that the loose fashions of the late 1920s were perfect for maternity wear. She probably spent most of her time in slip dresses with drop waists, or wrap dresses with loose tie jackets draped over them.

Although her home was in Cobham, Mummy felt she would like to be near her mother in Muswell Hill for the birth and so I was born a true Londoner, in a nursing home there.

'Never again,' she vowed after I came into the world on a sunny Sunday evening in July 1928. And so I remained an only child! It wasn't something I dwelt upon or even thought about, as there were several cousins and other family friends around me. Neither did I think about the fact that I had my parents' attention all to myself. I was just me, and here I was, happy.

TWO

Swansdown and Frills

Some of my earliest memories are of going to parties in Muswell Hill in North London wearing shiny patent-leather bar shoes and itchy organdie party dresses made by my mother, which were copies of the ones Shirley Temple used to wear in the films. Mothers everywhere were obsessed with dressing their daughters like Shirley Temple – and all the little girls wanted to look like her. I eagerly went to see her films at the local cinema, where a ticket cost 1 shilling and 9 pence. For us, it was incredible to see someone of our age topping the bill. Meanwhile all the mothers were studying where the seams were on her outfits.

I looked a lot like Shirley Temple, who was born in the same year as I was, 1928. I had a similar bone structure and complexion, and my hair was curly. What's more, the camera was interested in me from an early age. When I was four or five, a family friend, the actor George Relph, decided he wanted to take me to America and launch me as the English Shirley Temple, but this was definitely not what my mother wanted for her daughter. Mr Relph went on to greater things, including a role in one of the Ealing Comedies and another in *Ben Hur*, but I remained in obscurity, blissfully unaware of my missed opportunity. Hollywood somehow got by without me.

Meanwhile, my fashion-conscious mother dressed me to perfection and showed me off as her little princess at every opportunity. She made all my clothes on her Singer sewing machine – little dresses embellished with swansdown feathers and skirts with lots of frills. I even had a little swansdown bolero jacket. To complete the look, she put my hair in rags at night and, judging by the photographs, she also tinted it blonde.

The swansdown wasn't too bad, although the quill ends occasionally dug into me, but in all honesty I was never keen on wearing organdie. Its stiff, sheer crispness meant that it rubbed and chafed my skin. Still, I wanted to be dressed like all my friends, so I suppose it was an early lesson in suffering for fashion. The first of many! And we would do anything to look like Shirley Temple. Even the length of our dresses had to conform to her rule that hemlines be nineteen inches off the floor. According to the movie magazines of the time, her clothes designer at 20th Century Fox was of the opinion that the hems of small girls' dresses should reach just to their fingertips. Apparently, Temple was so accustomed to being fitted for costumes that she could tell if they were the right length within seconds, just by hanging her arms and leaning over.

It seems extraordinary now to think of a six-year-old dominating the worldwide box office, but the fact remains that she was Hollywood's biggest star during the mid 1930s. The film I remember best was *Bright Eyes*, which I probably saw in early 1935. It featured her signature song, 'On the Good Ship Lollipop'.

People who didn't grow up watching Shirley Temple films have trouble comprehending her appeal, I think. Her talent and magnetism are plain to see in YouTube clips – although it's a bit strange to watch her dancing around with grown men – but you have to place her in the context of the time to understand why she was such a huge draw.

She often played a poor little orphan, connecting her with millions of people who were either displaced or impoverished by the Great Depression of the 1930s. Her characters were innocent and trusting and saw the good in everyone, from millionaire misers to scruffy hobos. They could soften even the hardest heart with their child-ish capacity for love and compassion – and her films tended to have the kind of fairy-tale ending that everyone was dreaming of in those difficult, disillusioned times. So she wasn't just a chubby-cheeked child star who could sing and tap dance, she was a ray of hope and sunshine during very dark days.

At first, the economic crisis didn't really affect my family. The future was looking bright when, in 1929, the year of the Wall Street Crash, my father decided to set up his own coaching establishment for boys trying for university entrance. We left Thurlstone and moved to Chiltern Court, a house in Caversham, Reading, which my parents chose because it was easily accessible from Oxford, London and Cambridge. Chiltern Court worked well as a home and a school. It was a large nineteenth-century pile with decorated brickwork and ornamental chimney stacks, set in grounds that ran down to the River Thames, where we had a boathouse. There was a drive at the front and a spacious lawn; the large gardens at the back were full of trees and had a wide herbaceous border.

Six boys enrolled for my father's programme of tutoring, and suddenly my mother had a staff of six servants to oversee. I remember Brain, the butler (yes, that really was his name!), and Wilson, the cook, but the gardener and the others are a bit hazy. It's funny what sticks in your mind when you're a child. I can hardly recall the big family gatherings we had at Chiltern Court, the sports days for the boys or the long summer days spent lazing by the river. But one day a pigeon got trapped in a grating above the cellars and forever after I would plead with my parents in my baby language, 'Tell about me the pigeon!'

We led a happy and privileged existence, but it wasn't to last. It wasn't the Wall Street Crash that did for us – it was Britain coming off the Gold Standard in 1931, which came as a consequence of the crash and the depression that followed. I don't really understand what happened, or why. All I know is that 1931 was the year my parents lost all their money.

They soldiered on at Chiltern Court for a couple of years, but then the school had to close and we came down with a bump into a flat in Muswell Hill. It must have been a very traumatic time for them, but they didn't show it. I never had the impression that Mummy looked back with regret. She didn't seem to mind that we'd gone from having six servants to having no help at all. Like my grandmother Emily she had a positive outlook and just got on with things. She used to love moving house, so she was probably tickled to death when we landed up in the flat. She had a talent for making a stylish home, even on a budget.

Meanwhile, I was happily oblivious. Mummy was very good at inviting other children round and I had several little girlfriends in the area. There were lots of tea parties with jelly and ice cream, and birthday parties with a conjuror who would come with a top hat and pull things out of it. You took along a present for the birthday girl – a little heart on a chain, perhaps, a bracelet or a brooch – and we played blind man's buff, charades and pass the parcel, with its endless layers of brown paper to unwrap. There was also musical chairs and oranges and lemons, which was fun but a bit alarming if you were skipping under the arch of raised arms when it turned into an executioner's axe as the music stopped and you were out of the game.

Like children everywhere, we ate as many lollipops, boiled sweets, fudge and toffee as we could get down without being told off. Mummy used to make lovely dark treacle toffee. It was simply delicious, although quite brittle. Terrible stuff when I think of it – it would pull my teeth out if I ate it now. Coconut ice was another favourite and she also made melt-in-the-mouth peppermint creams from icing sugar, egg white and peppermint essence. You never see them now, so I made some a few Christmases ago as presents for people. Everyone loved them because they brought back so many memories – mainly of wanting more and not being allowed!

Appearances were considered very important when I was growing up. You were always on show in those days and you had to be well behaved. You couldn't run around and let off steam like the children of today. I can still hear my mother saying, 'Daphne!' in a loud, forced whisper. The tone of her voice was enough to stop me in my tracks – I knew not to go any further. Because I was an only child, she was probably stricter than most. 'I don't want you to be a little spoilt brat,' she used to say, because in that era children were to be seen and not heard.

So she was far from impressed when, at the age of four, I decided to cut my hair, taking a huge chunk out of my fringe. I can remember her displeasure all these years later. I expect I was just experimenting as many children do, but I didn't do it again.

Mummy made my clothes partly because we were not very well off, but in any case people sewed much more then than they do now. She also did embroidery and knitting. As it happened, I never wore hand-me-downs, but only because there was no one to be handed down from. I was the youngest girl in the family by far, what with my mother being the youngest of her siblings and my father being older. He was fifty when I was born. All my cousins, and even the children of my cousins, were older – therefore all their childhood clothes were long gone by the time I came along.

While I was having tea parties and wearing frills, at the other end of the age spectrum my older relatives were walking around in muted colours – there was a lot of beige – and holding lorgnettes up to their eyes. There were only a couple of fashion magazines then and just one 'look' every season, which everyone dutifully stuck to.

On my father's side of the family there were a lot of older women, mostly born in the 1870s. They were of tough Victorian stock and lived well into their eighties and nineties. Although they probably weren't as old as they seemed to me then, they certainly didn't dress young. Skirts were all below the knee. Not necessarily ankle-length, but no shorter than calf-length. No one wore trousers, apart from one of Daddy's sisters, who lived in the countryside. I only once wore trousers as a child that I remember, and Mummy never, ever wore trousers until her dying day. She lived to be ninety-five.

On my mother's side, my grandmother Emily was very proper in every way, including her style of dress. I wasn't exactly intimidated by her, but I was always on my best behaviour. She and her unmarried sister, Minnie, were now living in two adjoining houses in Rookfield Avenue, Muswell Hill, not too far away from our flat. Emily and Minnie were pretty old-fashioned, as you'd expect. They always wore longish dresses, long, loose coats and quite a lot of what I call 'lacy things'. They grew up in an age when people dressed 'properly'. You had your morning dress, your tea dress and your dinner dress – cotton in the morning, crêpe de Chine in the afternoon and velvet in the evening. By the 1920s it was relaxing a bit, but Emily and Minnie never really got into the modern era.

What would they make of the clothes I wear today? They probably wouldn't think I looked too bad, because I tend to wear longer skirts. My proportions are better suited to longer lines and I like flowing clothes, skirts that 'walk along behind me', as it were. I'm not very good in tight clothes. I've had to wear them, of course, but I'm never happy in them. I'm rather active and I like to kick my legs up. I split many a skirt jumping onto double-decker buses when I was young.

The 1930s silhouette was still slim, but it was far less boyish than it had been in the previous decade. Waistlines and fuller bosoms were back, thankfully for Mummy, who was starting to wear sleek jackets and matching narrow skirts, looking ahead to the styles of the 1940s. She always looked very feminine and in the summer she wore simple dresses in pretty printed fabrics. In the evenings, it was bias-cut, slimline floor-length dresses. The halter-neck was one of the new styles of evening dress, but I'm not sure how much she liked it because I never saw her wearing one.

Everyone wore hats, from bonnets to cloches, which had come into fashion in the 1920s and were still popular. Hats were statement features. They started conversations. In the mid 1930s, there was a return to Victorian and Edwardian styles, but in updated, sometimes startlingly modern incarnations. The back of a wide-brimmed hat might be adorned with a sweeping ostrich feather, for instance, but then cut out or pleated at the front to create an unexpected shape. There were lots of shovel-brimmed hats, pillboxes and hats with oriental peaks, jauntily set at an angle, often with a feather, bow or flower attached to the ribbon. Some looked archly stylish, others seemed to be announcing that the wearer had a sense of humour. And then there was the unashamed romance of the picture hats with their floppy wide brims, which you had to be quite tall to carry off. In short, there was a hat for every nuance of every possible mood you could be in. They were a fantastic form of self-expression. I still have a beautiful black straw hat of my mother's, which I treasure.

When Mummy went out in the evening, all she used for make-up was Pond's Vanishing Cream, a little face powder and some Bourjois rouge. She never wore lipstick and we hadn't even heard of mascara, which was strictly stage make-up. I don't recall anything to do with mascara until I was eighteen.

The generation above my mother barely wore make-up at all. They skipped the rouge and simply dabbed on a little powder with a swansdown powder puff. Things were so different – most people of forty looked quite old, even dowdy. I do remember the oldies wearing lots of jewellery, although it was nothing very flamboyant. They kept it to pearls, rings and delicate dangly earrings.

Restraint was a signifier of class, I suppose, which is probably why my uncle Gerald's wife, Janet, was not very much liked by the rest of the family. Uncle Gerald was a commercial traveller and he would bring my mother gorgeous handbags from wherever he had been. His wife, a hairdresser, went around with very bright red dyed hair and scarlet fingernails, which might have accounted for the frosty reception she received in those days of sensitive class boundaries and constant debate about who should mix with who. There weren't many people who looked like Janet in those days. She was very unusual and, although I was young, I was aware that she wasn't 'acceptable'. Perhaps if you were in the stage business she might not have seemed so outlandish, but I didn't have any connections with the stage then. Unfortunately, Janet got the thumbs down and that was that.

When he wasn't on his travels, Uncle Gerald lived just up the road from Granny; Mummy's eldest brother, Uncle Dickie, lived just down the road on the corner of Etheldene Avenue, in a large house with a beautiful porch that had ornaments on top, including an owl, still there to this day. Uncle Dickie worked for P&O shipping line and was married to Florence, a fragile and beautiful woman known to us all as Auntie Lolly. She was the sister of William Heath Robinson, the cartoonist and illustrator known for his hilariously over-complex inventions for things that performed simple tasks. During a visit to his house in Highgate I remember going up the staircase to the sitting room and seeing various strings to turn on the lights from his study desk and other contraptions to make life easier! But to me he was just an old man with white hair and I had no idea how famous he was for his brilliant, creative brain.

Dick and Lollie's daughter, Dora, was fifteen years older than me and often dressed in pretty floral dresses, but Gerald, their younger child, was the one cousin I had of my own age and we used to play together a lot. He was not very strong to begin with and rather overawed by his beautiful and clever sister, so he was pleased to have someone his own age to play with. He must have been devastated when Auntie Lollie died when we were seven years old, but I don't remember anyone talking about it. People just put their heads down and got on with things.

Christmases were always big affairs. We spent them at Granny's in Rookfield Avenue, where there were large family gatherings and lots of jollity. Families lived close to one another and saw each other more in those days, but the Garraways were perhaps even closer knit than most because they'd lost my grandfather.

On Christmas morning I'd wake up fizzing with excitement. Had Father Christmas been? In my stocking I'd find a tangerine and all sorts of bits and pieces, little books and puzzles – nothing much at all, but everything to a child. We walked or went by bus to Granny's house. It wasn't far and I'd be skipping all the way.

It was good fun at Granny's because there were always a lot of us, although not many children – sometimes only cousin Gerald and me. We spent most of Christmas Day in the dining room making our way through the huge traditional meal of turkey and all the trimmings, which included tinned tomatoes thickened with breadcrumbs, stuffing, roast potatoes, sprouts, sausages and bacon. After all of this there would be jellies and cream for the children and Christmas pudding for the grown-ups, with the brandy lit well away from us young ones.

As the only young girl there, I was rather adored and probably spoilt, despite my mother's best efforts. Mummy's lovely older sister Gertie lived in nearby Winchmore Hill and so she and her husband, Otto, and their children, Adrian and Diana, also spent Christmas at Granny's. Otto only had one eye and wore a patch – how he lost it, I do not know, but it didn't stop him working as a watchmaker and an organist. He had come over from Germany and changed his name from Klimpsch to Kingsley, which was sensible after the First World War when Germans were not much liked here. He used to go back to Germany on business and always returned with handmade toys and dolls for me. I still have Jennifer, the blue-eyed china doll he gave me. All the best dolls were from Germany, I was told.

Another toy I loved was Joe, a donkey on wheels. I spent many happy hours being pulled along on Joe, usually by my older cousin Adrian. Joe even lasted long enough for my son, Mark, to ride, before he eventually rotted away. Ben the dog, also on wheels, was another favourite, although not big enough to sit on.

Cousin Adrian, despite being seven years older, was marvellous at playing with me. He built a swing in his garden for me and showed me how to communicate with a cat's whisker and a tin – a makeshift telephone that conveyed sounds over a taut extended wire by vibration. I thought he was amazing, and he *was* amazing. But years later when I went back to the house, what had seemed like a fantastic jungle with a lake and trees had shrunk to a small suburban garden.

I don't remember having many Christmas presents, but I suppose all the relatives gave me something. Little trinkets of jewellery, writing paper, a new drawing book, a pen or a doll. We used to collect cigarette cards, which were used to stiffen cigarette packets and advertise the brand. They had pictures of footballers on them, or of movie stars, flowers, pets, coats of arms, city views, military dress – everything you can imagine. There could be twenty-five to a hundred in each series and the key was to collect the whole set. Of course, we children didn't smoke, but all the adults did, so we were constantly cadging their cigarette cards. It was wonderful to be presented with a whole set at once, which only ever happened at Christmas.

My father was now teaching at a school in Cockfosters run by a Mr Henley, who was very supportive of Daddy and recommended him for a better job at St Peter's, a school in Weston-super-Mare, miles away in Somerset. So Daddy went down there on his own to teach and look for a house, while we stayed in Muswell Hill. With my father so far away, it must have been a comfort for my mother that our top-floor flat in Summerland Mansions was quite near my grandmother's house.

From the windows of the flat I could look out onto the street below and see the muffin man ringing his hand-bell to attract customers as he walked along with his wooden tray of muffins on his head. Across the road was a baker's shop with the unusual name of Monnickendam, which had a very foreign ring to me. I had no idea it was the name of a town in the Netherlands.

I remember the large sitting room and the grand piano at the far end where my mother used to play and sing. For some reason I didn't like her singing and would crawl under the piano and cry, which must have been rather disconcerting for her! I remember that we came home one day to discover that the kitchen ceiling had fallen down. This was a disaster for me as the tempting bowl of stewed gooseberries ready for my supper was full of bits of plaster. It must have been much more of a disaster for my mother, but these things never really ruffled her. She just got on to the maintenance man about having it repaired as soon as possible.

My father, when home, used to take me for walks in Alexandra Park. We would go to Alexandra Palace, with its huge entrance hall and eucalyptus trees. I can smell those trees now – a minty sweet pine mixture. We'd walk around trying all the pinball machines and then look into the shooting gallery, where men lay on the floor firing at the targets.

Outside on the grass one day, my father put down his trilby hat and a huge woolly caterpillar walked onto it. My father knew the names of practically everything: insects, flowers, trees, the lot. He was a walking encyclopedia and later on he used to make up general knowledge papers for students and correct exam papers, so it was always fascinating to go anywhere with him.

Daddy had seven brothers and sisters and some I knew better than others. I don't remember meeting Leonard, who was supposedly the 'black sheep' of the family for reasons unknown to me, and I only recall the thick white hair of Arthur, who was a district commissioner in Nikuru in Africa. But Daddy's eldest brother, Percy, is vivid in my memory. It was Percy who was on holiday in Lowestoft with my father when he met my mother for the first time, and he was my godfather as well as my uncle. Percy had a moustache and a very deep voice. He was always immaculately dressed with a gold watch chain across his waistcoat and grey spats over his black polished shoes. He also carried a black, silver-topped cane.

On my birthdays he would give me a pound and the amount of years in shillings as well, which was thrilling. He and his wife, Ida, used to take me to tea at Derry & Toms (it now houses a branch of Marks & Spencer, as well as other shops) in Kensington. They were both very kind and I enjoyed my outings with them. If the weather was nice we would go up to the roof garden, which is still there today, complete with trees and flamingos. At the time it was the largest roof garden in Europe. Intrigued, I would watch as Percy took two tiny white pills out of a little box in his pocket and put them in his tea. Saccharin, of course!

Ida was large and imposing, at least to me. Her hair was like an enormous puffed-up brown meringue on her head. It must have taken ages to achieve that mountainous effect – and a terrible bother to get washed. She wore voluminous skirts and, like Percy, had a deep, booming voice. She was every bit as likeable too. Many years later, after Uncle Percy had died, my last sight of Ida was in a tiny room in the Distressed Gentlefolks Home in Vicarage Gate, Kensington. It seemed to me a sad comedown for such a formidable lady, now a shadow of her former bombastic self.

Of Daddy's sisters, the two I came to know well were Violet and Olive, both spinsters, who had been volunteer nurses in the First World War. They were very different from each other. Auntie Violet lived in Chelsea and went frequently to the theatre and concerts. Auntie Olive lived in Spaxton in Somerset with her friend Amy and several dogs.

Auntie Olive walked around in huge, loose tweed

suits and wore her hair in an ordinary bun. She was very mannish, now I come to think of it. She looked like my father and the Selfes were not a very good-looking family. They were all very masculine in appearance, even Auntie Violet, who had a hooked nose.

I used to go and stay with Olive and Amy in the school holidays. The house was very cold. There was no central heating and the electricity was powered by a shaky old generator that was housed in a shed in the garden. When the lights began to fail, Olive or Amy had to go out there and wind it up to get it going again.

We spent the days walking in the wooded countryside around them, with its little streams and masses of primroses, aconites and kingcups. We'd pick bunches of wild flowers and fill a large bowl on the table near the huge bay window that overlooked the garden. One day I was invited to go as a beater on a shoot. Auntie Olive lent me a pair of brown corduroy trousers – the only trousers I remember wearing as a child. Inevitably, they got quite muddy on the beat and she was so cross when I got home because things were very hard to clean and it meant washing by hand. But the fact remains that if you go beating, you're going to get a bit grubby.

My first school was St Martin's Convent in Page's Lane, Muswell Hill – it was nearby and I did quite well there, though one day I must have taken a dislike to it because I ran home at lunchtime. Crossing the Broadway was tricky even then, so it was not a commendable thing to do at five years old. 'Such a nice man brought me across the road, Mummy.'

It was enough to make any parent's hair stand on end and I don't think my mother was too pleased. What's more, I think the school was turning me into a Catholic, which she did not approve of, so when I was eight I was sent to board at Westcliff School in Weston-super-Mare, which had been recommended to my father as a suitable school for me. It seems a young age to venture away from home, but I happily accepted it as something that was entirely normal and took it in my stride. I was quite excited, in fact. With a father for a teacher close by and having lived at Chiltern Court, the school environment felt very familiar and I was completely comfortable with it.

I really liked being at Westcliff because I enjoyed being around people and having other children to talk to. I had lots of good friends there. I'd never felt lonely as an only child, because I'd never known anything else, and I didn't wish for a sibling. But I was very cheerful and outgoing, just like my mother and grandmother, and for a sociable only child a boarding school proved to be the perfect place.

THREE

Scarlet Cloaks and Big Knickers

School knickers get a bad press – especially the old-fashioned ones we wore in the 1930s and 1940s. But there were definite advantages to the high-waisted, elasticated pants I ran around in during my school years. They were warm in the winter months; they kept you covered up when you did handstands; they didn't shift around when you were doing sports; and you could tuck your handkerchiefs inside the leg elastic. My grandmother Emily could only have dreamt of having such practical undergarments when she was growing up. Not that she would have dreamt anything of the sort, of course. Heaven forbid.

Like outerwear, underwear changed radically in the twentieth century. Before that, it was pretty primitive, and in the 1850s my great-grandmother would have been walking around in ankle-length cotton cambric bloomers under her hooped skirts. These had two separate legs joined at the waist, which is why they were known as a pair of bloomers or drawers – and we still talk about a pair of knickers or pants when they are clearly a single garment. They weren't particularly comfortable –

it depended on the weave and thread count – but at least they came in different colours, including pink and red.

By the 1870s, my grandmother would have been lucky enough to be wearing bloomers with legs that were properly joined up, perhaps even in softer fabrics like silk, flannel and muslin. These started rising up the leg as hemlines got shorter – knee-length frilly cami-knickers came in during the 1900s and silky slimline Directoire knickers, elasticated at the knee, were all the rage as the dress silhouette narrowed around 1910. Then, during the flapper age, French knickers arrived, presumably from France, although in Paris they were known as *culottes en soie*. These thigh-skimming shorts were shockingly brief for the time. Made from silk – and sometimes lace – their open-leg style, free from elastic cuffs, meant they were good to dance in and didn't show under dresses. Mummy loved them, but I suspect that Granny left well alone.

In the 1920s, as clothes became more diverse, there was an explosion of underwear styles and fabrics. Granny might have stuck with her long silky bloomers, but for everyone under the age of forty, there was now such a thing as *lingerie*. New materials like rayon – known as artificial silk – helped to bring about a revolution in knickers, as did nylon. People shudder at the thought of nylon pants now, but they were easy-wash, quick-dry, non-iron little miracles of their time.

I, of course, knew nothing of lingerie. In the 1930s I was racing around the grounds of Westcliff School wearing big school knickers under a dark turquoise serge tunic and cream blouse, with a girdle round the waist – a girdle in those days being a belt with fringed ends, like a boy's cotton pyjama string, only wider. This was our everyday wear, washed once a week in the school laundry. When we went to church or out on Sundays, we wore hats and tailored fawn coats, with peacock blue shantung dresses underneath. I remember mine had pleated collar and cuffs. It was a very attractive uniform, although I am sure I didn't appreciate it at the time. I wore it constantly during term time for the next five years, so it must have become rather boring. As far as I can recall, I never wore my own clothes at Westcliff, even at weekends.

School life was a whirl of physical activity. In one corner of the lawn was an extremely climbable tree with a labyrinth of branches that started low down the trunk. We spent many hours clambering up it and dangling upside down from its boughs.

I learned to swim in the Knightstone Baths down in the town, with floats attached to me. They were like weird metal kettles – round tin things that would bounce about in the water on either side of me, getting under my armpits. I was very glad to get rid of them once I could stay afloat unaided.

Like underwear, bathing costumes had been shrinking

fast over the previous decades. Victorian bathing dresses and bloomers had made way for figure-hugging tops over long shorts, which in turn became the one-piece. Year by year, the shorts became shorter – so the costume I was wearing when I learned to swim bore a close relationship to the ones we wear today. The difference was the fabric, which in my day was a light knitted wool that sagged and became heavy when wet. But swimwear technology was about to make huge advances as manufacturers caught on to the benefits of rayon and nylon.

It was great to be able to swim, but the water at Knightstone Baths was not heated and it was a relief to get out most of the time. We were given a sticky bun afterwards, and a cup of cocoa to warm us up. The sugary drink and snack were very quickly demolished! No one was figure conscious or thought about diets then. We used to eat all sorts of things like Yorkshire puddings, treacle sponge and tea with cakes, but we didn't get fat, I don't know why. Some girls were obviously bigger than others but I don't remember anybody being overweight.

We didn't swim in the sea as it was never near enough – the tide at Weston goes out a very long way, leaving a huge expanse of sand and mud. The nearest we got was in winter, when we dashed in and out of the waves that crashed over the promenade. Sometimes we played hockey on the beach, from where you could see the aptly named islands of Flatholme and Steepholme. In bad weather we could hear the boom of the foghorns across the bay at Watchet.

We often climbed the hundred steps leading up to an old Roman encampment behind the school. It was a wonderful place to play, carpeted with beautiful wild flowers and plants that grew on the chalk up there. We would bring back samples to study and paint in class. In hot weather we had lessons outside – every pupil's dream! The blackboard would be put at the top of the lawn, which had quite a steep slope, and we'd sit on the grass a little way down. On one occasion somebody removed the wedge from under the foot of the blackboard without the teacher knowing, so when she went to write on it, the whole thing collapsed down the slope. She was not amused, but we were! It was one of the highlights of the school year. In Form III B, we had some strong and forthright characters in our midst and we were always getting into trouble.

I don't remember missing my parents, but of course it was lovely to see them at the half-term break. Every Sunday I would write letters home, and my father and mother would write a letter each to me that I would receive in the week and read with pleasure. Eventually my father found a house near the school where he was teaching – St Peter's – and my mother left our Summerland Mansions flat and moved to Weston-super-Mare. The new house, Greyfriars, was large and imposing, with a wrought-iron veranda and huge cellars. We didn't use all the rooms but we sometimes played games in the cellars, although it was a bit spooky down there. I spent many happy hours dressing up and playing in the garden. Like so many girls I dreamt of having ponies, and my father's top hat came in handy for a riding outfit. The only thing I lacked was a horse, but at least there were donkeys on the beach in the summer. I did a lot of racing up and down the beach on donkeys. I always had my favourite, usually the biggest one, as I was tall for my age.

Everything was going well: I was happy at school, my mother liked living in Weston-super-Mare and my father enjoyed teaching at St Peter's. My grandmother and uncles would all come for visits and it was a carefree time. Then, out of the blue, the lovely headmaster of St Peter's had a heart attack and died aged only fifty-three. This was a really great blow for everyone and was to have unforeseen consequences for us in particular.

As second in command to the head, it was assumed that my father would take over the headship, but for some reason I never discovered, he was pushed aside and another man stepped in. Daddy was so upset that he decided to leave. He was well known and liked in the profession and through his old friend Mr Henley he was eventually appointed to the boys' prep school Ludgrove, in Wokingham, Berkshire. So it was another move for my

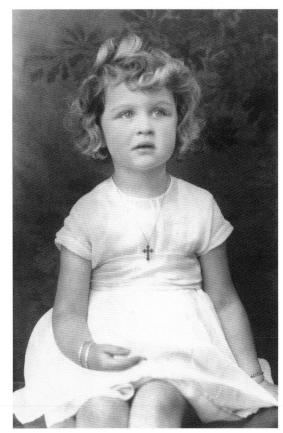

1. My father, Francis, in a nice tweed jacket.

2. My mother, Irene, in her 1940s suit.

3. Me, aged three, ready to party!

4. At Chiltern Court,
Caversham, in 1931,
à la Shirley Temple.

5. Outing to Stratfield
Saye, 1932, where I fell
over and landed in newly
laid tarmac, dirtying
my pink suit.

6. Me at Weston-super-Mare, 1936. This ride was the beginning of my obsession with horses.

7. Skipping along Weston's promenade in 1936.

8. Dressing up and looking the part in Daddy's top hat, 1936.

9. Wearing proper riding gear (at last!) on my horse Gavotte in 1948.

10. One of my first modelling shots in the 1950s.

11. A studio shot from the 1950s. Thankfully the parrot was fake, but that didn't stop the claws from being incredibly spiky!

12. A profile shot from the 1950s.

13. My wedding day, Bexhill, 1954.

14. Jim and me with Mark on his toy donkey, Joe. I had always made my own clothes and I was particularly pleased with this dress.

15. With our pet fox, Vicky, at Haslemere.

16. Jim with Mark, Rose and Claire on a family outing to West Wittering in 1961.

parents, this time to Wokingham, while I stayed on boarding at Westcliff.

My school consisted of four big Victorian houses, two of which were commandeered by the Army at the outbreak of war in 1939. Half the school was evacuated to Wales, which was considered the safer option, but only wealthier families were able to send their girls away. My parents couldn't afford it, so I stayed as one of only eight boarders along with the day girls. It was a time of real freedom, because the adults looking after us were understandably distracted by the war and didn't keep as close an eye on us as they usually would.

We had lots of outings – picnics on the Quantocks, Brean Down and Cheddar Gorge – always setting off in the same direction past the Air Force camp at Locking and the pottery there, with its low flat-roofed buildings. One of my friends, Guelda Tothill, lived at Uphill, just outside Weston. It always amused me that her name and the place she lived were alike. She shared a tiny house with her mother, who gave us lovely teas when we went there on a Saturday outing.

Having the Army on the doorstep was marvellous for the school staff – our gym was used for staff dances, which the soldiers were invited to, and one night members of Joe Loss's Jazz Band came to play. This was a really big event and caused great excitement among us girls. Eddie Conn was leading the band and he was a huge celebrity in our eleven-year-old eyes, like a modern-day pop star. Our bedroom windows backed on to the playground near the gym at ground level, so that night we climbed out to see what was going on and managed to get autographs of the band (I still have them!). We were thrilled, but Matron was not pleased to find that we had sneaked out of the dorm and we got a severe telling-off.

The headmistress, Miss Aldwinkle, although strict, was really very nice. She had a nephew, Aylmer, who flew a Hurricane aircraft and he would come down to visit her with his friend Leslie Graham, who flew a Spitfire. These clever, handsome pilots would read us bedtime stories, which we found incredibly exciting. The story I remember the best was *Moonfleet* by J. Meade Faulkner. The book belonged to my friend Jean Ellis, who actually lived at Swanage, Dorset, near where *Moonfleet* is set. Is that why it especially captured my imagination? Certainly my adventurous nature was stirred by tales of pirates and smuggling. I used to daydream about dodging excisemen and discovering hidden diamonds.

In the years that followed, I often wondered if Aylmer and Leslie had made it through the war, because the survival rate for pilots was frighteningly low. So I was pleased to learn recently – quite by chance – that Aylmer had gone on to lead a full life as a commercial pilot. Perhaps I'll find out what happened to Leslie one of these days!

Cocooned at Westcliff, the war really didn't have much of an impact on me. Nearby Bristol was badly bombed and we spent many nights sleeping in the cellars, but this simply provided grand opportunities for midnight feasts with tins of Nestlé's milk and chocolate biscuits. I was happy and outgoing and had lots of friends. It's no good being a retiring violet at boarding school.

When Mummy came down to visit me at half-term she would stay at the Welbeck, a little hotel on the front. Sometimes she brought Granny's help from London, a cheerful, chatty lady named Gladys, a real East Ender who had pretty much become one of the family over the years. Gladys always wore a soft felt hat and raincoat on these trips, and she would usually be carrying a shopping basket. Other times Mummy came with Else Blytt, a Swedish schoolteacher who was billeted on my parents during the war. Daddy didn't come very often because it was difficult for him to get away from school. I missed him, but looked forward to having an exciting weekend with Mummy, walking on the promenade and beach. In those days photographers would take photos as you strolled along the prom. They posted the pictures on a board and you could go and buy the ones you liked. I have several of these to remind me of that time.

It was always a treat to go for tea and a knickerbocker glory at the Odeon cinema cafe. One day we were sitting at our table and Mummy picked up a bottle of orange squash to shake it and pour us a drink. What she didn't realize was that the top was loose and when she shook it the contents went everywhere. The poor waitress had a lot of clearing up and my dear mother was aghast.

In the holidays, I went home to our new house in Wokingham, Dawn Mead, where we stayed for the next fourteen years. It was an Edwardian house with a beautiful big garden that Daddy tended lovingly. I remember it cost a thousand pounds to buy and we had to rent it for the first year while my parents saved up. There was no talk of mortgages or loans. They had to wait until they could buy it outright.

Much to my delight, we acquired a dog. A friend of my mother's had died and no one knew what to do with her Pekinese, so of course my mother said she would have him. Bobby turned out to be the most sporting lapdog you could ever imagine, and was a faithful friend for many years. He bounded along with us on our country walks, leaping over the deep grass and bracken to keep us in sight, and in the evenings he snored contentedly on the hearthrug. I'm sure he thought he was a much bigger dog! He was, in fact, quite big for a Pekinese, and you certainly knew when he sat on your lap.

We also had a tortoiseshell cat called Patch, who would cautiously come to meet us when we returned from a walk, never venturing further than the pillar box at the corner of Forest Road. Both Bobby and Patch were subjected to my penchant for dressing them up in my doll's clothes, many that I made myself. Once they were dressed, I'd push them about in my doll's pram – and they were surprisingly amenable to this treatment. Bobby wasn't always placid, though. When someone told my mother that the bluey-grey mud at Weston-super-Mare worked wonders as a face pack, she had to try it. So, after a visit to me at half-term, she duly took some home to Wokingham and put it on her face. Poor Bobby didn't recognize her and growled and barked until she took it off!

I sometimes went to stay with relatives or friends in the holidays. Mummy's older brother Frank and his wife, Winifred, used to give me a wonderful time – I stayed with them in both Eastbourne and Alfriston in Sussex, where they lived in mock Tudor-style houses, which were all the rage. Winifred was a frantic whirlwind of a person and a holiday with her was full of exciting things to do. But, my goodness, you had to mind your Ps and Qs. She was a real tartar. As long as you behaved, she would take you everywhere, introduce you to all sorts of interesting people and make sure you had friends to play with. She even took me riding, oh, joy! But you had to be punctual and polite at all times. No elbows on the table!

It was the same when I went to stay with my god-mother, Winifred Bentall, the daughter of Leonard Bentall who founded the Bentalls department store in Kingston, still there today. The Bentalls lived at Oakwood Court, a large country house also in the mock Tudor style near Leatherhead in Surrey. It had a big terrace and gardens and a long meadow with an archery range. I vividly remember their shining Rolls-Royce with its wonderful leathery smell. Tapper, the chauffeur, lived in the stable block next to the house and always seemed to be washing the car. He was very cheerful and diligent, never without his uniform and cap.

Mrs Bentall, Leonard's wife, was petite and quietly spoken. She wafted around in a cloud of lavender and was kind and generous, but you had to behave yourself around her. Children in those days were still expected to be quiet until spoken to. You very much did what you were told – the very first time you were asked. Needless to say, I felt more relaxed when I went out with Winifred, just the two of us. She used to take me to Bentalls for tea in the elegant restaurant, where my mother had once sung at the *thés dansants*. I used to love sitting at a table with Winifred, nibbling cake while the orchestra played.

I was growing up fast. At thirteen, I was ready for a change of schools. It seemed logical to move me nearer home – and, as it happened, there was a school close by that my mother had long ago set her sights on for me. When my parents lived at Chiltern Court in Caversham, she had noticed groups of schoolgirls walking around in dramatic long scarlet cloaks. *How stylish*, she'd thought. The girls were from Queen Anne's School, Caversham, so she duly noted it as somewhere I might potentially go. Of course, her hopes were dashed by the 1930s crash and the move to Muswell Hill – but now here we were again, just outside Reading, with Queen Anne's very nearby.

My mother's dream came true and I was duly accepted for Queen Anne's, although I didn't get a scholarship, as hoped. Oh dear, I don't know how they afforded the fees. It must have been quite an effort. It helped having Else as our lodger – and Mummy was now employed as an undermatron at Ludgrove School so that she could supplement Daddy's wages. Schoolteachers weren't paid much, so she had to do something. During the Second World War, it became increasingly common for women like Mummy to work, so it was perfectly acceptable socially. After working for the Bank of England during the First World War, it must have felt like a case of another war, another job!

I started as a boarder at Queen Anne's in September 1941. Being an only child, my parents thought it was better for me to board, and there were hardly any day girls in the school then. I settled down quite happily and always enjoyed school. The only time I remember being upset was when I was told that my cousin Adrian had been killed in Italy at Anzio during Operation Shingle. Adrian had been very kind to me when I was younger and

I was desperately sad to hear of his death. Everyone in the family was devastated.

Reading had quite a lot of bombing during the war but somehow up in Caversham we didn't suffer much. We probably heard the noise from our dormitories at night but I don't remember ever having to go down or outside. We always had air-raid practice, in case, though – and I'll never forget the glow in the sky over faraway London during the Blitz, as buildings exploded and burned.

Our uniform was navy, red and grey, and this time my big school knickers were bright scarlet. In class, we wore navy-blue skirts and white shirts. For games, we had cream cable-knit sweaters to keep us warm – as well as the red cloaks for going between the buildings. Usually you had a second-hand cloak, as the new ones were very expensive, and there was a 'bank' of leftovers, because most people when they left school didn't take their red cloak with them. I certainly didn't take mine as it was so old by then, but I've very kindly been given one by the school, quite recently. It's made of heavier material than the one I had in the 1940s and it's a darker red, but it's a similarly striking garment that conjures visions of magic, sorcery and secret societies, if you're imaginative in that way.

The school had about 400 girls until halfway through the war, when Putney High School was evacuated on to us from London and we suddenly had an influx of new girls. There was a lot of rearranging but it seemed to work all right and we all squeezed in. Everyone who was at Queen Anne's during the war remembers Sunday suppers of cold meat and beetroot. Wartime rationing meant that each of us had a little jar with butter in it, two ounces to last the week – likewise sugar – and woe betide you if you ran out before the end of the week – dry bread!

The staff sat at the high table at the end of the hall and we sat at long tables down the room. 'No scraping of chairs when you get up or down, please! Always lift your chair!' The headmistress, Miss Elliot, would say grace: 'For what we are about to receive, may the Lord make us truly thankful.' She was very fierce and strict and we were all in awe of her. If you misbehaved and were sent to her study, you would quake outside the door, dreading the sentence.

Our gym and games teacher, Miss Bradley, was her complete opposite – young, blonde, talented and very inspiring. Her enthusiasm was infectious and we all adored her. I nearly took up PE as a profession because she was such an excellent role model and teacher.

We had a large games field. In the winter we played lacrosse and hockey, wearing red tricolene shirtwaister dresses with sleeves. These were very short for those days – above the knee – and they were worn with a white canvas belt and red knickers. Lacrosse was new to me, but

I managed to get a place in the second team. Unfortunately, during one match a girl scooped up the ball and one of my front teeth with it, which over the years has been added to and replaced more times than I can remember. My mother was more upset about her beautiful daughter losing a tooth than I was. It never made me feel self-conscious. I was just a schoolgirl and not particularly concerned about my appearance.

At the top of the field we had hard tennis courts where we played in summer. I was quite a reasonable tennis player, but some of the others were really brilliant. I was better at cricket, mostly as a slow bowler. For tennis and cricket, we wore the same outfits we used for gym – grey flannel divided skirts, red Aertex polo shirts and again the red knickers. Everyone had three of everything, so they could be washed regularly. We played matches against Wycombe Abbey, Downe House and other girls' schools. Fortunately for me, there was a lot of emphasis on physical exercise, because I was an average student academically. We played games every afternoon, and matches on Saturdays. Every morning before breakfast we would go for a run round the field and there were country runs at weekends or on afternoons when there were no games.

There was a swimming pool on one side of the quadrangle. It was very nice in summer, but even then it was jolly cold with no heating at all and, although it was roofed in, my memories are of feeling absolutely freezing. I took my Bronze Lifesaving exam all right, but had to forgo the Silver as it meant staying longer in the water and I was just too cold to stand it.

Ballroom dancing classes were held in the assembly hall and, as I was tall, I always had to be the 'man'. This did pay off in later life with the real thing, although I retained a tendency to lead when it should have been the man. We also did Greek dancing, wearing suitably Grecian-style white tunics, although I have no idea why. It seems a strange option for an English girls' boarding school, especially in the middle of a World War. During the classes we ran and skipped around the room and sat on the floor to do arm exercises – 'pushing the clouds away'.

In the senior school, we used to have dances and sometimes the boys from neighbouring Leighton Park School would be allowed to join us. What fun that was for an all-girls school! Many romances ensued, with furious letter writing and note passing. Well, we considered them romances, but they never got any further than the note passing. I think even our games mistress, Miss Bradley, was swept up in the excitement. She took a shine to the games master from Leighton Park, who occasionally taught us as well. He was a marvellous gymnast, I remember, like an India rubber ball.

When I first arrived at Queen Anne's, our 'dorms'

consisted of five or so beds to a room, but later on we had rows of single cubicles with partitions and doors for more privacy. Brilliant for feasts and reading under the bed-clothes. I joined the Girl Guides, which was something that most girls did in those days, including the Princesses Elizabeth and Margaret. The uniforms were very smart, with lots of military-style details. We wore felt hats and neck scarves fastened with woggles, or ties and tie pins. Our dresses had wing collars, epaulettes and button-down pockets, and we sewed badges onto the arms after performing various tasks. It was nothing like the Girl Guides wear today, which is far more practical but nowhere near as smart. There have been several uniform revamps over the years and now they're wearing two-tone polo shirts with zips, leggings, jeans and patterned skirts. I shudder to think what my leader would have thought of them; she was a real stickler for keeping our uniforms smart.

I managed to get into the Queen Anne's school choir, which had quite a good reputation. We did lots of concerts at the school and joined the Reading Youth Choir to perform at the town hall on special occasions. One notable concert was performing *Faust* with some famous singers in the main parts, including the contralto Kathleen Ferrier. I still have the programmes, of course. I am such a collector that I can't bear to part with things.

The school had its own chapel and we went to a short service twice a day and three times on Sundays. A few years ago, we all went back one May open day for Old Girls. Several of us, including Sheila Hogarth – one of the few who I still keep up with today – piled into our old pew for the anniversary service and giggled together as we had done when at school – nothing had changed except for the grey hairs!

We all wrote letters home on Sundays after Chapel and in the afternoon we would go for a walk around the local roads and countryside. Sometimes we'd wander up St Peter's Avenue behind the school, where our old house, Chiltern Court, still stands. I think I remember it better from passing by during my school years than I do from the time we actually lived there, when I was only two or three. During the war it was used by the Ministry of Agriculture and Fisheries. It is now owned by several businesses – the front lawn is a car park and the gravel road outside has been tarmacked over.

In the sixth form we did domestic science with Scottish Miss Blair. We used to go to a separate building across the road from the school to bake scones and little cakes, do housework and laundry and all sorts of things that students don't get taught now. We even learned how to wash up correctly. Glass and silver first!

There were serious shortages to contend with because of the war, though. The wartime spirit was instilled into us at school, and we found ways of making do and saving everything. I'm sure that being eleven when the Second

World War began must have affected my attitude to life. We were taught to make the best of everything and it came through on all levels: food, dress, behaviour, what you could and couldn't do. It amuses me to see articles in the papers today about 'ways of saving money' – that is how I have always lived. It's nothing new.

We had dressmaking and crafts in another building in the school grounds, where we learned to sew, weave and knit. It seemed to take ages to finish anything as it was only one class – albeit a double period – each week. My first effort was a bobbly blue seersucker blouse, which I was quite pleased with. Then I wove a red wool scarf that I still have, seventy years later. It would be a long time before I embarked on a coat or anything as complicated, but it was there, in the crafts building at Queen Anne's, that my lifelong love of sewing and making clothes first began.

FOUR

Riding Hats and Hacking Jackets

My biggest love as I was growing up was horses. I don't know where it came from, as my mother and father were not in the least horsey, so I was a bit of a rogue. But by the time I was fourteen, I was so mad about horses that I simply had to persuade my parents to let me have riding lessons. It took a terrific amount of persistence and wheedling, but eventually I was allowed to start going to a stables near Emmbrook, just down the hill from where we lived, run by George Vincent Francis, known as GVF. To begin with, I was mostly taught by GVF's assistant, the rosy-cheeked Angela Gough. No pony for me to start on, as I was too tall, so I was given Brown Owl, a sixteen-hand brown gelding, as quiet as you please.

Clothing was rationed from 1941 and you had to have coupons and cash to buy everything, so most of my riding gear was second-hand. Since furnishing fabric wasn't rationed at first, people started making their clothes out of upholstery and curtain material. Parachute silk was highly prized, I remember. Women up and down the country were getting married in recycled parachutes if they were lucky enough to get hold of them. If not, they were walking down the aisle in pretty, lightweight sofa fabric.

Good-quality shop-bought clothes were expensive and hard to come by, so when we wanted something new, we often cut up old things. Mummy managed to look very smart all through the war because of her skills with her Singer sewing machine. She wore dresses or tailored jackets and slim skirts – in wool or tweed – which she either made or adapted from her pre-war wardrobe. Blouses were trickier, though. Rayon crêpe was very much in fashion and it was far easier to buy something in crêpe than to make it.

Meanwhile, my father had very long arms and could never buy shirts with long enough sleeves, so they had to be made for him. In the village of Emmbrook, not far from where we lived on the Reading Road, we found a Mrs Ottaway, who made beautiful shirts. I always remember going to collect them from her tiny cottage. Mrs Ottaway was of an indeterminate age, very thin, wore her dark hair in a bun and dressed in flowered wrap-around overalls. A little later on, we found a dressmaker in Reading who made things for my mother and me.

I wasn't really conscious of what Mummy wore until the war, and then I mostly remember her in pinstripe suits and calf-length tea dresses. She also had a lovely brown lace evening dress at one point, too. She dabbed perfume behind her ears and the smell brings back the war years to me more than anything. It was Coty L'Aimant, and I bought it for myself in the 1950s. She also wore a Bourjois perfume that came in a dark blue bottle – Lily of the Valley, which I don't like. Still, she didn't have much choice, as there wasn't a lot of perfume about in wartime.

Midway through the war, the Utility Clothing Scheme was launched, which was good news for everyone. It was the point at which the government acknowledged that poorly made shop-bought clothes were a waste of resources and factory space, as well as being bad for morale. In those days, we expected our clothes to last. It's so different from now, when people throw away and buy new, and you can get a T-shirt for £3.

The big fashion houses were already producing utilitarian clothes when several top London fashion designers were asked to submit designs for the government-backed Utility Clothing Scheme. They had to conform to strict regulations about how much material and how many buttons were used, so it was an interesting challenge. Hardy Amies, Norman Hartnell, Victor Stiebel and Worth were among the designers who participated, and the result was a line of simple but elegant coats and dresses in surprisingly good materials. These started selling in the shops in spring 1943 and Mummy bought a really well-cut utility suit in soft navy wool.

Vogue magazine praised the 'revolutionary scheme' for giving women the chance to buy 'beautifully designed clothes suitable to their lives and incomes'. All the same, fashion pretty much stood still during the war. Although the Paris fashion houses didn't close down, luxury was out of reach for all but the very few – and, with most women wearing uniform, utility and occupational outfits, there wasn't much room for experimentation. Hats were always a good way of brightening up a drab outfit, especially as hat material wasn't rationed. Feathers, flowers and veils on hats became all the rage. But when it came to high fashion, everyone was waiting to see what would happen when the war ended – if it *ever* ended.

I wasn't thinking about clothes, though. All I cared about was horses. Of course, the equestrian world had its own strict style code, but this relaxed during the war through necessity. At first I wore jodhpurs and lace-up shoes when I went riding. Later I had some breeches, which I wore with long socks or gaiters and ankle boots. You needed a button hook to fasten the gaiters, but they were more protective than socks and so worth the effort. Ankle boots, I discovered, were very comfy and less restricting than long boots. I had to get boys' boots to go with the gaiters, as they didn't sell them for girls. Actually, they were army boots and cost 43 shillings and 6 pence.

I bought the breeches new at the Bedford Riding Co. in Bedford Street, London. They had wide 'wings' on the side – quite a period piece now! There were no stretch fabrics, so they had to be roomy above the knee to allow for movement – and tight below the knee to enable a secure grip in the saddle and prevent chafing. They looked like something only a pantomime character would wear these days, but they were very smart in their time.

Bearing in mind that I wore trousers just once during my childhood – while on the pheasant beat at Auntie Olive's – I naturally enjoyed the freedom that came with wearing jodhpurs. Riding apparel suited my tall frame and wide shoulders. I liked the clean, masculine lines of equestrian clothes. But I had very long arms, like my father, and so my tweed hacking jacket had to be made to measure at Heelas of Reading, our nearest big department store, requiring a hefty outlay of cash and coupons.

Earlier in the century, hacking jackets had been long and columnar, mirroring the dress silhouette that became so popular in 1910. They were often double-breasted and reached midway down the thigh, which can't have been terribly practical. Thankfully, they were revamped in the 1920s and the shorter jacket was born – my jacket was just the right length, with two slits at the back. It was a snug, trim fit, with smart square shoulders, and I was very pleased with it. The basic riding silhouette for women hasn't changed much since, because it hasn't needed to.

When I had become reasonably safe in the saddle, I started hacking round all the local lanes and woods. I didn't have a hat – not until Uncle Percy very kindly bought me a bowler from Lock's in St James's Street – so I wore headscarves, or nothing on my head at all. I was given lots of 'stocks' – neckwear – by an old hunting friend of the family in Wokingham, and string gloves were also useful, as they helped to keep a grip on the reins in the wet.

GVF was a well-known and respected figure in the horse world and I went to lots of shows to watch him and his fellow riders winning coveted awards. His son, Dick, was in the Air Force, stationed at Brackley in Northamptonshire, and the sight of him in his uniform was always dazzling. He looked so handsome and debonair. However, he was much older than I was and had a pretty girlfriend called Mary, so it was very much a case of worshipping from afar. After the war he became the famous novelist Dick Francis, writing crime fiction about horses.

I read horsey books avidly and knew the names of all the well-known riders and horses of the day. I could never afford a pony of my own, but this didn't stop me scanning *Horse & Hound* every week and dreaming. I went to all the local shows, tagging along with my friend and neighbour Beryl Brown, who had her own pony. I remember watching the various families riding and jumping, desperately wishing I were one of them. In those days you had to own a pony to join the Pony Club, so I could only look on wistfully.

The Moss family seemed to win everything. Mrs

Moss, a formidable, large-built woman, was an accomplished rider. Her children, Stirling and Pat, had perfect ponies and always looked fantastic, immaculately turned out. Although I didn't personally know them, I was very much aware of them and their impressive mother. Stirling, of course, later became a very famous racing driver.

Another family that rode in all the shows and took a lot of prizes were the Pullein-Thompsons. The mother – another redoubtable figure – wrote forty-eight books about horses and ponies under the name Joanna Cannan, and one of her daughters, Josephine, wrote around fifty, many of which my friends and I eagerly devoured. When Josephine died in 2014 I came across her obituary. Once asked why so many girls are passionate about ponies, she replied, 'They need something to love, to nurture. It keeps them off pop stars!' She was right on all counts.

I used to get to the local horse shows on my bicycle, or sometimes Beryl Brown's parents would take us in their car. Wartime meant that nobody went very far afield – my parents had an old Hillman car that sat in the garage unused throughout the war years. Every morning, my father cycled to Ludgrove on his big Raleigh bicycle. Meanwhile, Mummy would pedal her Hercules the mile or so to Wokingham to fill her bike basket with food from Parmentiers, the grocer, at the corner of Station Road. It was about a mile uphill to Wokingham, but satisfying to whizz downhill on the way back, through Emmbrook and uphill again to our house!

Mummy worked hard during the war years, but at least she had help. After Daddy retired from Ludgrove in 1943, he started coaching boys for Common Entrance and we usually had at least three boys living in, so she couldn't have managed on her own. We had a maid, Edna, who was just sixteen when she came to us. Edna was fair and gawky and would blush at the slightest thing, but was friendly and willing to learn. I can see her now in her white cap and apron over her black dress, stockings and shoes. She came in daily and did a lot of housework, but not the washing and she wouldn't scrub the floor. She cleaned the silver and did the dusting and other things like that. For the rough work, we had another 'treasure', Mrs Jewel, who would do anything – all the menial day-to-day work of running a home. She was a warm lady with a gruff Cockney voice.

We had no washing machine, refrigerator or dish-washer in those days – a terrifying thought now! The nearest we had to a fridge was a little metal larder with wire mesh doors that sat on the shelf in the main larder. In hot weather we would put it outside in the shade. Milk bottles stood in pans of water with a cloth over the top to keep them cool. If you didn't cover them, the blue tits would peck off the metal tops, especially if they were left outside for too long after the milkman had delivered them. Everything had to be covered up, even in the larder. We used muslin covers with beads round the edges to stop flies getting in.

The whole kitchen was painted dark green, the fashion of the time, which made the room quite dark – and the brown tiled floor did nothing to brighten it. Next to the kitchen – known as the scullery – was the morning room, a light, cosy room with a window that looked out onto the lawn and our bird table. In those days, the blackbirds loved the porridge my father scraped out of the saucepan for them each morning. Now they seem to have got very fussy and don't like porridge any more. Is it the porridge or the blackbirds that have changed?

The dining room was at the front of the house, which also served as a sitting room and had comfy armchairs, thick orange velvet curtains at the windows and a 'Cosy Stove'. On a table in the corner there was a wireless radio. In winter, we spent most evenings in this room listening to a very funny show called *It's That Man Again – ITMA* with Tommy Handley – and other wartime programmes. Daddy would read and do the crossword and Mummy would sew or knit socks. In summer, we were always in the garden.

During the war we didn't change for dinner, unless we had guests or went out. On special occasions, such as Christmas or birthdays, or when we had guests, we would use the drawing room. It was a handsome room running the length of the house, but although we had a fire in there it always seemed chilly. The piano was against the near wall but, even so, practising was a very cold business, which explains why I never progressed very far. In the winter it was a job to keep warm even with an itchy angora bolero over my stiff organdie party dresses. I spent those evenings longing to go upstairs and put on a thick jumper over a cotton blouse. To this day, I can't bear to wear fabrics that itch or irritate for long, even in the name of fashion. I still can't wear angora or mohair – I'm not a wool person. Thank goodness for man-made knitwear.

With no central heating, the windows of my bedroom would frost up with ice on the inside, making incredible lacy patterns. I was glad of my warm winceyette pyjamas and bed socks, although I went off hot-water bottles after mine burst one night and I got badly burnt all over my tummy. There was a fireplace in my room, which was only ever lit when I was ill with the common childhood diseases of the time, such as chicken pox or measles or mumps. It was lovely to lie in bed watching the firelight shadows on the ceiling. When I had mumps I was put on a blissful diet of ice cream, though I could have done without the stiff neck and swollen glands.

The bathroom across the corridor, like the kitchen, was painted dark green – and was therefore dark – and the lino on the floor was particularly chilly to the feet. It was the very last place you wanted to go during the night! We all wore dressing gowns and slippers. During the war, baths could never be more than five inches deep and I'm still very abstemious with hot water. I never have a deep bath – I'm just not used to it. Outside the back door we kept pet rabbits in a hutch and when they died we used to cure the skins and make slippers or mittens. My father showed me how to pin the skins flat on a board and rub them with alum to preserve them. It's not a skill I've used in recent years, but I'm glad I still know how. However unlikely it seems, you never know when these things will come in handy again. Carpentry, for instance – Daddy taught me all my carpentry and many years later, when I had my own home, I made a wardrobe. It was a lean-to and I made it from scratch. I haven't got an electric drill any more although I wish I had, because I could do with one around the house, frankly.

Our surroundings were quite rural and Daddy and I frequently roamed the coppice opposite our house looking for wild flowers, plants and any animal life we could find. All sorts of beetles lived among the fallen trees and undergrowth. Finding a stag beetle was quite usual then. My father taught me a great deal about wildlife and plants and I was never afraid to pick up spiders, beetles or worms. I also learned to put a swift end to cockroach grubs and wire worms in the vegetable plot by squashing them between finger and thumb. Sometimes we would go up Chestnut Avenue to pick blackberries, and one day we found an adder. We weren't frightened but we didn't touch it, just admiring its markings as it slid away into the bushes.

My father loved his garden, and so did I. Our gravel drive at the front of the house led to a lawn edged with Syringa bushes. At the side of the house was a huge espaliered white cherry tree. It was a constant battle, even with several yards of net curtaining, to keep the birds from eating those delicious cherries. The back lawn was bordered on one side and at the end by rose pergolas and arches. We were always going off to the little wood on the other side of the road to find replacement poles, as they seemed to rot very quickly.

Outside the kitchen window was a small orchard that my father planted with different apple and pear trees. Beyond that was the wide vegetable patch, where all our vegetables were grown with the help of the curiously named Earwicker, our gardener, who did a lot of the digging. He was like a little brown gnome, but a tireless worker. Beyond the vegetables was the big orchard of Worcester Pearmain apple trees. Every season we put white collars and sticky bands on them to keep the bugs away. Beside the orchard were two asparagus beds. When the asparagus was in season we would have great platefuls of it with melted butter and brown bread, a complete supper in itself. After the asparagus had gone to seed, it grew into a beautiful fernlike forest and I have happy memories of playing hide-and-seek in it.

My own tiny patch had lavender edging and I grew various annuals. Alongside the path we had a thick cypress hedge and towards the top of our garden was another circular lawn, the garden shed and a little woodland patch with a few silver birch trees and a lot of bulbs in the spring.

At the edge of the lawn was a marvellous Victoria plum tree which was sometimes so weighed down with fruit that we had to prop it up – further trips to the wood opposite to find suitable branches to use! My mother just loved plums and there was an endless supply of them raw, cooked or in jam – although you had to be very careful when picking them not to get stung by wasps. The plum tree hid the compost heaps on which my father grew marrows and beyond them was a lavender walk with its big old woody bushes arranged along a little winding path, under which one could surprise a lizard or two in the hot weather.

The boundary of our garden looked onto a narrow strip of land that stood between the railway cutting and us. The cutting was so far down that the trains could hardly be heard. Occasionally we would climb on the fence to see the Silver Jubilee or the Flying Scotsman hurtling past. It was still the age of steam, so all we usually saw of them was the plume of billowing white smoke as they raced by.

We were very firm friends with our neighbours, the Armigers. They were a lively and sociable couple and we had a special hole in the laurel hedge through which we could slip into their garden. Mrs Armiger was like a rosy apple and always cheerful. She kept chickens at the end of the garden and often gave us eggs. They had a quince tree too and every year my mother made quince jelly.

The Armigers had a tennis court and I can remember many tennis parties there with friends. My father being a very expert tennis player meant he was always in demand. We had a lot of fun playing croquet on the lawn outside our drawing room, too. My mother was always impatient to get on and win and was an excellent cheat in the nicest possible way, which used to make us laugh.

Our neighbours on the other side were a family with two girls who were so shy it was very difficult to make conversation, if you could get them to talk at all. They were excellent needlewomen and later the older girl went to work at the White House in Bond Street, which specialized in white linen blouses and lingerie, where she was a great success.

Opposite us lived a lady called Maud, who had been a court dressmaker and now worked from home making church vestments. We would inspect her latest elaborate embroidery commission with awe – she was a true expert. Maud lived with her friend Kathleen, a secretary in the Civil Service. They had a tiny garden full of miniature plants and ornaments, and you had to mind how you walked along the little paths for fear of trampling things. Both women were also tiny in stature, eschewed make-up and wore sober clothes in the muted colours of the day. But they did have their hair done regularly. We used to go to their house to play whist and other card games and to join their little supper parties. Parties were not very lavish during the war, but that didn't stop us having fun. I had a party dress I was particularly fond of – it was tartan taffeta and very pretty.

Further down the road from us were two elderly sisters who enjoyed holding tea parties in their lovely big garden. They were probably not all that old, but they seemed ancient to me. Eva was very thin and always wore pale blue; Mabel was portly and favoured more sludgy colours. Then there was Miss Flack in a large house on the other side of the road, all by herself with her golden retriever. She was an outdoorsy type, with flushed cheeks and short brown hair. She dressed in rust-coloured tweeds and constantly took her dog for walks.

Down the lane beside the coppice near our house lived Mrs Povey, whose French husband we did not see much, and her daughter Yolande, who was never dressed as stylishly as one expected a girl who was half-French should be. Yolande seemed lonely and I liked her company, so we used to ask her to come and play. I will never forget the hot summer's day she came round to our house wearing a thick, hand-knitted vest under her dress. The dress was rather ordinary, but the vest, which was knitted in multi-coloured stripes, was quite a sight. My aghast mother soon got her out of it and hastily put it back on her before she went home! She always had the most unsuitable clothes, poor Yolande.

Several times during the holidays I spent the weekend at the home of my school friend Ann Tibbs, whose father was vicar of Lynchmere in Surrey and knew lots of interesting people, including Richard and Dilys Dimbleby and their two young sons. Richard Dimbleby, the legendary journalist and broadcaster, was the BBC's first war correspondent before he went on to be its top TV news commentator. David and Jonathan followed in their father's footsteps, of course, and are still broadcasting today. Ann had horses and ponies of her own and we would go to the local shows and ride around the countryside. My dream finally came true when I got to take part in the local gymkhana. I don't think I won much, if anything, but it was tremendous fun. Ann's brother David was a real wizard at winning on his little pony. Her dark, handsome elder brother, Michael, was in the Navy, and on the rare occasions he came to visit Ann at school we were all very keen to meet him. Like Dick Francis, he looked dashing in his uniform and we'd gaze at him adoringly, although I don't think he even noticed.

Ann was great company and knew how to tell a good story. My favourite of her anecdotes was about Professor Joad, the celebrity philosopher and broadcaster who was a regular on *The Brains Trust*, a wartime discussion programme on the BBC. He used to live near the vicarage, and one day, Ann was out riding with him when it began to rain. Naturally, she put on her jacket for protection, but Professor Joad took his off.

'It's raining. Don't you need your coat?' she asked him.

'I don't want to get it wet!' he replied, stubbornly folding it up. A wonderful eccentric!

When I was sixteen, I managed to pass my School Certificate with Matriculation. In other words, I had enough credits and a pass in Maths to get 'Matric', which would have enabled me to go to university. But I didn't fancy that. Not many of us did in those days. Girls did nursing, occupational therapy, teaching or just got married. I didn't fancy any of those, either. Working with horses was all I wanted to do, but I knew it would be a tough job persuading my parents that it was a good idea.

The end of the war was a happy distraction from thoughts of the future. For a short while, all that mattered was that the past was behind us. I was a member of the

Girls' Training Corps (GTC) at school and there was great excitement when we took part in a victory march through Reading. Joining the GTC was a very constructive experience. We learned car maintenance, Morse code, signalling and all sorts of useful things – along with less beneficial skills like endless marching in the quadrangle, 'becoming as one'.

The fearsome Mrs Coxwell-Rogers drilled us relentlessly. 'When you slow march, your beret [or was it your belly?] should shake!' she would bark at us.

Imagine us on the victory march – schoolgirls – sandwiched between American policemen wearing white caps, gloves and putties, many of them at least six feet tall, leggy and gorgeous! Not to mention the other serving Army and Navy personnel. It was fantastic, the talk of the week.

When I left school in 1945, aged seventeen, my games teacher and my mother talked me into doing Swedish Massage – 'The Thing' in those days. This was the moment I learned that your parents, while wanting the best for you, *might not actually know* what's best for you.

I said I would try it, and after a successful interview at the Swedish Institute in South Kensington I duly started the course. However, although I liked the practical side (handy with my big boyish hands!) the theory was beyond me. I had not done enough Biology or Chemistry up to the standard required and I just could not keep up with the other girls, who knew so much more. So, after several frustrating weeks, I left and finally managed to persuade my parents to let me make a career with horses.

GVF advised me to become a resident pupil at Colonel R. E. Pritchard's (REP) Riding Academy at Nepcote Lodge, Findon, near Worthing in Sussex. Nepcote was an attractive Victorian house and garden with stables surrounding the big yard and a spacious indoor school. Now the whole thing has been pulled down and a housing estate built there – at least retaining the name Nepcote.

To begin with, the course was full, so I helped REP's son, Peter, with his stable of showjumpers. I was a long way from being Elizabeth Taylor in *National Velvet*, but I just loved it all. It was very hard work living in the head groom's cottage. There was no electricity and it was freezing when I got up by candlelight at five thirty every morning, with ice on the inside of the windows, to muck out and groom the nine horses. I used to stuff newspaper down the insides of my jodhpurs for extra warmth. On really cold days it was a treat to take the horses that needed shoeing to the farrier in Findon, where I'd have a few moments to warm myself by the forge fire.

Peter was kind and good to work for but, like his father, very particular – not a single straw left on the yard when you swept, straw in the boxes neatly arranged up the walls, everything just so. I spent many hours raking the sand and sawdust mixture level in the indoor school.

At nine o'clock it would be breakfast in the main house under the wing of REP's wife, 'Mrs P'. I learned how to down a bowl of porridge in double-quick time in order to get the horses and myself ready for the ten o'clock ride.

I didn't ride much to begin with, but Peter provided me with horses when I joined the next course properly. While I worked for him I would accompany him to all the shows as groom and general dogsbody, for 10 shillings a week. I became adept at plaiting and bandaging and fixing Mordax studs to the showjumpers' horseshoes. There was hardly a show around our area that we did not attend. Richmond and White City and Windsor were the big ones, but Christchurch was one I particularly remember, mainly because it poured with rain all day long. We were absolutely sodden and the wind blew everything away. Fixing the Mordax studs that day was no joke, but there was no complaining. Eventually we went home in the horsebox in dripping wet clothes, glad to be out of the storm.

Our everyday riding kit was a shirt and tie, a hacking jacket and jodhpurs, unless it was hot and we didn't wear a jacket. (By now I had a second-hand riding cap, bought for 30 shillings, plus the bowler that Uncle Percy had bought me.) If you had long hair you tied it back. Nobody wore their hair all over the place like they do now. My hair was quite short and it was naturally wavy so I didn't have to do much to it. It did its own thing.

My parents paid £74 a term for the instructors' course. We rode in the covered school every morning and everyone put a lot of effort in. The 'Old Man' (as REP was known) was 'Weedon trained' (at the rigorous British Army School of Equitation in Weedon, Northamptonshire) and very tough on us. One morning, my horse, Canny, ran away with me and he shouted furiously, 'You ought to be in a cart under a pig net!'

How we put up with this kind of treatment I don't know, but it was probably the making of us and we learned quickly. I often think it toughened me up for the rigours of the fashion world and modelling (which at this point I had no idea was to come my way). Riding is a discipline, just like anything else. You have to be organized, punctual and wear the right clothes. You look after the horse first and yourself afterwards, but in order to look after a horse you've also got to look after yourself.

REP had dressage horses, including one particularly good one called Harlequin, with whom he spent many hours training. This horse lived in the No. 1 box on the other side of the yard to Peter's lot. Once, while we were putting down rat poison in the lofts above the stables, I inadvertently missed a beam and put my foot through the ceiling of Harlequin's box. Luckily, the horse was out, but I never heard the end of it!

Shortly afterwards, Peter gave me a little grey mare called Silver to ride. She was quite a madam and bucked me off every morning – it became a ritual and we all laughed and got on with it. Once she settled down, she was fine and perfectly manageable. We all fell off regularly – except for one girl, Vera, who was pretty experienced and eventually became the Old Man's assistant. She and I became friends and had some fun together in the evenings, going down into Worthing and buying fish and chips to sit on the beach and eat out of newspaper.

When we had completed the six-month course, we went to Billy Smart's place at Winkfield, near Ascot, to take our exam in the big covered school there. It was a nerve-racking day. Just before the exam, several of us went to the local inn nearby and bought ourselves a small cherry brandy to help fortify ourselves – and most of us passed, I'm glad to say. After passing a written exam too, I became a proud qualified riding instructress with 'I of H' after my name. It stood for Institute of the Horse, which is now the British Horse Society.

I was at Nepcote over the dramatic winter of 1946–7, the year of the big snow. Everything froze solid and we couldn't go anywhere. Luckily we had the indoor school, so the horses didn't suffer too much from lack of exercise. In February 1947, while we were piling on woollen jumpers and wrapping ourselves in scarves, news came through from Paris of Christian Dior's 'New Look', which was instantly recognized as a revolution in fashion. With its pretty suits and dresses – tight waists, full skirts, high heels and little tiny hats that perched on the top of your head – it was an entirely new fashion silhouette that turned its back on rationing, utility and sombre colours. I remember seeing the first pictures in the newspaper and gaping gleefully. It was such an extravagant change, a revelation after the severity of earlier 1940s fashion and the restrictions of wartime. Paris glamour was back, with a vengeance.

The New Look was all about longer, fuller skirts that required lots of material – but how on earth were we going to do it? Clothes rationing wasn't lifted until 1949, so at first we couldn't do too much – we just lengthened what we had! I was delighted when Mummy's dressmaker in Reading was able to make me up a New Look pale blue corduroy coat with silver buttons. I wore it for many years, eventually dying it black to make it a bit 'smarter' to wear in London. In those days you could send things off to be dyed professionally at Clark's of Retford to give them a whole new lease of life – it was much cheaper than buying anything new, and a lot less effort than remaking it from scratch. That dressmaker also added a huge black border to an emerald green dress I had worn at school, which meant that it and I were able to see a lot more good times together.

I was at Nepcote for eighteen months in all, including the instructor's course. In that time, I helped to look after all Peter's horses. One chestnut gelding, Passport, was very tricky and would bite or kick at any opportunity, although eventually he got used to me and began to behave decently. He was a bit of an old crock when Peter acquired him, but with patience and slow work he became a very good showjumper. I was sad when he went to a new home. Watchman was a big brown horse but he had a more placid nature – he was a real pleasure to 'do'. I became fond of them all.

Meanwhile, I came to realize that Peter, although much older than I was, had taken a shine to me. This was my first 'romance', at nineteen years old, which might seem late to girls nowadays, but was entirely normal then. Peter was attentive and I thought him rather a dish, but nothing ever developed, although at one point he did think he might like to marry me. However, it wasn't to be and eventually I left Nepcote to start my first job, teaching riding at Rosemead School in Littlehampton, Sussex.

The stables were actually in Arundel, by the station – not very palatial, but the horses and ponies were well cared for and I was lucky to make a valuable friend in the other girl working there, Liz Weatherall. I had digs at a Mrs Mason's opposite the Norfolk Hotel in Arundel and Liz was staying with her grandmother in Middleton-on-Sea, which wasn't far away. The rides were generally with schoolchildren up on the Downs nearby and we had some lovely times. Once we went on an all-day ride up on Stane Street, the old Roman Road. Another time I had to take a horse to Bognor, so I rode all along the beach from Littlehampton, which was breathtaking. They were happy days and Liz and I had some fun in the evenings, going to the sports club in Middleton and out to the Black Rabbit, a well-known pub just outside Arundel on the river.

We made a lot of friends and I remember one evening going to my friend John's house in Middleton, where Charlie Kunz, the pianist, was playing. By then, I had a boyfriend – David – who dealt in cars. I was keen to learn to drive and I had my first experience behind the wheel in a big red Alfa Romeo that he was selling. Being a car dealer's girlfriend meant that I drove a variety of shiny cars around the Sussex lanes. I wouldn't recommend learning to drive at night in a fast sports car, but somehow I got the hang of it. Eventually I took my test back in Reading, after having the requisite twelve lessons at the British School of Motoring.

On the day of the exam, I got in the car with the instructor beside me and off we went around the exam route. After some minutes, he put his clipboard away and sat back. Oh dear, I thought, he is not going to bother any more. I must have failed.

Still, I kept going. 'Why did you give up on me?' I asked him, when we arrived back at the centre.

'I didn't have to worry, because you are a very decisive driver. You have passed,' he replied. What a relief to get that over with and have my freedom on the road. For a worthy job with horses, it was essential to be able to drive. To celebrate, I went out and bought myself a pair of smart leather driving gloves.

FIVE

Boned Bodice and Sequins

The first evening dress I made was terribly dashing. It had a puce slipper satin skirt and a black lace boned bodice covered in little gold sequins. You couldn't buy strips of sequins in 1948, so I sewed each one on individually. It took ages, but the effect was wonderful, so shimmery and sparkly. It was like walking around with your own personal spotlight.

My mother taught me how to make a boned bodice and I can still do it, although there's not much call for it these days. Strapless then was much more decent. Strapless now I wouldn't touch, even if I was young, because I don't think it's very flattering. It's not boned or anything. It's often unsupported and it doesn't do anyone any favours. I'm amazed by some of the horrible strapless dresses people wear on the red carpet. All that bosom on show looks dreadful!

I wore my slinky, glittering, home-made evening dress – and long black satin gloves – to the Horse and Hound Ball at the Grosvenor House Hotel in Park Lane. I was there with my friend Anne Linfoot and a big group of friends from Essex. I had been hunting with the East

Essex – and occasionally with the Essex Union – for a year by then, and my dress couldn't have been more distinct from my hunting outfit, which was a black jacket, breeches and long boots, a tie or stock and a bowler hat. (Only the hunt servants wore 'pink'.) It was a complete transformation and I was rather pleased to be able to show off a different side of me to my hunting pals. The evening was terrific fun. One of our party, 'Tiger' Davies, won the Hunting Horn Contest for his exceptional blowing.

I had left the little riding school in Arundel by this time and teamed up with Anne Linfoot, a friend from the instructor's course at Findon, after she rang up one day to say she was starting a riding school and livery stables on her father's farm near Braintree in Essex. Would I like to come and help her run it? It was a splendid opportunity, so off I went to Braintree.

Looking back, I realize that I only spent about a year with Anne, but we packed so much into it that it seemed far longer. Her father had a big farm at High Garrett, just outside Bocking. He also owned the stables to a big house occupied by Barnardo's, further up the road, and this was Anne's domain. The business instantly took off. Anne had lived in the area all her life and was well known and liked, so our services were in demand. Our Sunday-morning ride became very popular and many of the older pupils became our friends.

It was a very happy time. I loved the unpredictability of working with horses, even though it could be hazardous. Our usual morning ride around the villages near Stisted involved going past the slaughterhouse and the piggery, neither of which horses care for, to say the least. Most of them could be persuaded past, but sometimes it was quite a battle with a new horse. I was thankful for being naturally strong – and it was an excellent way of warming up on a cold morning.

We did fairly well at the local shows. I can't remember winning much, but I have a few rosettes somewhere, proving the point that it's the taking part that's important! We had a very swift and handy gymkhana pony called Lex, who won a lot of prizes. Anne's older brother, John, rode a chestnut mare called Gay, who pulled like a train but on whom I had some fun, although not a lot of success at showjumping. I wore hunting gear for showing horses, with a topper in place of a bowler when I was riding side saddle.

Anne rode her horses in the local point-to-point, but I couldn't join in, as in those days a 'paid servant' was not allowed to. I helped with the schooling and made the best of it – there was plenty of scope for practising in the huge fields on the farm. I think I must have felt a bit hard done by at the time – an outsider again – but I've since wondered whether this archaic rule might just have saved my life, for reasons that will become apparent.

We managed to hunt most weeks – Anne on her black gelding, Patrick, and me on 'my' bay mare, Gavotte. After Anne and her father got some horses over from Ireland, I was first out on a brown mare called Kitty at a meet of the East Essex. Kitty was a pleasing ride, but hadn't done much hunting. Soon after starting out, we jumped a ditch so erratically that I was deposited in it, much to the amusement of everyone else.

Having remounted, I thought she would be all right at the next, a wooden gate, but although we stayed together, the gate did not – more red faces! It was October and the ground was cold and hard, so I was very glad of my bowler hat, just in case – the correct headgear for hunting and the safest hat you could wear. Legend has it that the man who designed the original bowler a hundred years earlier – Edward Coke, the brother of the 2nd Earl of Leicester – tested its strength by stamping on it twice. The hat remaining intact, he paid 12 shillings for it. After her ignominious start, Kitty eventually became a trusted and reliable hunter – not very fast, but safe – although I rarely rode her without my bowler.

One morning in November, as I was saddling up our little pony, Merrylegs, she took exception to it and kicked me on the forehead. Oh dear, blood everywhere, while Merrylegs galloped off. I found Anne and in no time at all was taken to the hospital and stitched up. Much to my embarrassment, when I arrived at the hospital and had to remove all my clothes, I was wearing my scarlet school sports knickers. The ones from Queen Anne's! I still had them because they were so nice and warm in the winter, but no amount of explanation could stop the nurses giggling. Amid the blushes, I comforted myself that at least it wasn't a case of, 'Red hat, no drawers!'

I recovered pretty quickly and in December we went to lots of dances and days out hunting again. Initially I wore my hair in a fringe to cover the scar left by Merrylegs's kick, but in time it faded. My father and mother were more concerned about it than I was, I think. They came over and spent Christmas at the White Hart in Braintree to check that I was all right, while discreetly making sure that life with the Linfoots was all that it should be.

In the evenings, Anne and I regularly played darts at the local pub, which was always fun. I was pretty skilled at getting my arrows where they were aimed, although the maths involved was quite another thing. We went to hunt balls in Chelmsford and Colchester several years running, and to private dances. There was always something to look forward to and dress up for. We even had a horseback fancy-dress party on one of our Sunday rides, and I won first prize for an Eastern Princess costume! As well as making and sewing my evening wear, I customized dresses that friends gave me when they tired of them. I borrowed some dresses, too – although I couldn't borrow Anne's as she was much smaller than me.

I picked up some helpful tips from my mother's magazines – *Woman & Home*, *Woman's Weekly* and *Home Chat*. These were funny little black-and-white publications printed on thin paper, not the glossy magazines they are today, but they were full of advice about how to make something old look new with a length of ribbon and a silk flower. They included free patterns for clothes and knitwear that we could send off for. But I bought my Simplicity, Butterick and, occasionally, Vogue patterns in Reading.

From time to time I would see a copy of *Vogue*, but Mummy never bought it as it was too expensive. Instead, people passed magazines around to friends in their circle, sometimes with a note pointing out page references for this and that, so I was aware of the beautiful evening dresses Victor Stiebel and Hardy Amies were producing, even if they were far out of reach.

Anne's brother John and I went out together quite a lot. He had a steady girlfriend, but she didn't hunt or come to the hunt balls, as it was not her thing and she wouldn't have been comfortable. And when John went up to London in the January of 1949, I went as his companion while she was busy working. It was very platonic and although I liked John very much, I wasn't going to steal someone else's boyfriend.

We stayed in a hotel in Bloomsbury – separate rooms, of course – and from there we ventured out for a taste of London life. My little suitcase didn't contain much: a blouse, a skirt and a dress, none of them New Look. It was all very well for the Parisiennes to say that Christian Dior had brought the joy back to fashion after the war, but along with all that joy came the headache of reinventing one's wardrobe and finding whatever material one could to produce longer hemlines and fuller skirts. Fortunately, I wasn't fashion conscious enough to worry too much about it yet. I wore a coat and hat, of course, and gloves. Always gloves and a hat! I had a lovely red felt hat with a brim for that trip.

John and I ate out at Lyons Corner House and went to see Walt Disney cartoons at the Cameo Cinema. One of the highlights of our stay was seeing a musical revue called *Starlight Roof* with Vic Oliver, Pat Kirkwood and Fred Emney at the Hippodrome. I wore an afternoon dress, as we were not very grand, but it was still a far cry from the farm and horses.

I went home to Wokingham for Easter, where I caught up with my friends, visited my aunt Minnie in Winchmore Hill and made time for riding some horses for Charlie Budd, a local dealer friend of GVF. In June, Anne and I went with a big party to the Derby, my first time there. I backed first, second and third – My Love, Royal Drake and Noor, forever etched on my memory.

I made a new outfit for the occasion, a turquoise linen suit that took a long time to finish as I only really had evenings free. It had a pencil skirt and a separate longish peplum top with a high, round neckline and elbow-length sleeves. Again, the skirt wasn't flared, mainly because I saw this particular pattern in the shop and liked it – and, of course, it looks better to team a slim skirt with a long jacket. I wore it with a small white hat trimmed with a veil, white gloves and white court shoes, and I thought I was the cat's whiskers.

I left Anne's stables after getting a call from REP's son, Peter, who had now married and moved to Ditchling in Sussex. The deal was that he would let me have a horse to myself and I could go to shows with him. This sounded too good to be true and I jumped at the chance. Luckily, Anne agreed that it wasn't to be turned down, so off I went in September 1948.

Peter and his wife, Dulcie, had quite a bit of land in Ditchling and it was fun getting it all going and looking after the horses. But time passed and no riding materialized, let alone a horse. I became adept at doing jobs on the farm – stooking and harvesting, making a rick and occasionally driving the new Ferguson tractor – and I made some friends in the village. However, it was not furthering my career with horses, so reluctantly I decided to call it a day and go home to my parents. It was my first experience of promises not being fulfilled, and it proved to be a valuable lesson for me. It taught me to keep positive and move on to the next thing.

Meanwhile, Anne and I stayed good friends for the next few years and I often went to visit her and her family. I expect we would be friends now if she hadn't died in 1953. A horse threw her while she was practising her jumping for a point-to-point. It was a tragic, untimely death, and a reminder of how very dangerous riding can be. Anne was an extremely good rider, so it could happen to anyone – and sometimes I wonder whether I would have made it to my eighties had I been allowed to compete in the point-to-point when I was twenty.

After leaving Peter and Dulcie, I had to earn my keep while I was living at home. The big question was, how was I going to do that? A friend of my mother's worked at Heelas of Reading, a department store now owned by John Lewis, and he said he would put in a word for me there. He must have said the right thing, as I started as a sales girl in the 'coats and suits' department on 29 November 1948.

I was still mad about riding, so most mornings I rode Charlie Budd's horses at six and then cycled the seven miles to Reading, arriving at Heelas in time to change into my uniform and clock-in at eight forty-five a.m., shedding my coats and waterproofs in the cloakroom. I used to cycle in with my friend Avril, who lived nearby.

She wasn't my closest of friends, but we both liked having a cycling companion. We cycled home again at half past five and then I often went out in the evenings to meet friends, go to a club or a milk bar – all the things one does at the age of twenty, when one is brimming with energy and excitement! The Reading Road was a well-lit, inhabited route, so I never minded cycling home in the dark, although sometimes I took the bus or got a lift from a friend.

It didn't matter what you wore to work in the store, as long as it was brown. I had a two-piece suit made by my mother's dressmaker in Reading. It was a New Look outfit, with a long skirt and a little peplum jacket, but in a rather inferior material. Mummy could have made it, but she was already run off her feet looking after the boys at home. She couldn't do everything!

Working at Heelas was terribly busy too. There was always something to do. I tidied the stock – because customers were always messing it up – ran errands, took orders from customers and saw about parcels that had to be sent off. There was a lot of writing things down. If somebody was ill, you would be sent to cover for them. You talked to the customers – in those days people did talk to customers – showed them the stock and made suggestions. Most were nice – although some were nasty – and the idea was to have a satisfied customer, not one who was going to bring something back. We always used to say, 'If it wasn't for the customers, we could manage very well!'

We sold Alexon, Eastex and Windsmoor coats and suits, Berkertex dresses and jackets and Pretty Polly and Horrockses dresses. A Horrockses dress cost around 4 guineas, a Goray skirt was 31 shillings, a silk or voile blouse was between 50 and 60 shillings and a suit or coat cost from £7 to 8 guineas. People wore long coats then much more than they do now because they didn't have cars. You were always on a bus or walking, so you needed something substantial to keep you warm or dry. All the girls at Heelas had at least two coats – one for summer, one for winter – and a raincoat. My pride and joy was still my pale blue corduroy New Look spring/summer coat, which I never tired of wearing.

I always used to pick out my favourites when the new stock came into the store. I do the same when I go for a fashion shoot now. I'll see something on the rail and think, I'd like to wear that one! Sometimes I do and sometimes I don't – it depends what the photographer wants, of course.

Our head of department at Heelas, Mrs Kay, encouraged us to go through the new stock, as it meant we got to know what we were selling. She was a lovely lady of about fifty, but she was strict. You did as you were told. She invariably wore a Hebe suit, often in tweed, herringbone or grey wool. It was a very recognizable style, with the skirt pleated back and front, and a little jacket with a collar and buttons. Everybody had them, including me.

It was at Heelas that I finally got the hang of the New Look. We had a staff discount and in my lunch hour I'd browse the dress department to see what they had. Most hemlines were well below the knee – calf-length – and New Look-influenced. Mummy didn't much go for flared skirts, but I loved them. The older generation tended to stick with square shoulders, boxy jackets and slimline skirts, while we younger ones defined ourselves with a fuller skirt silhouette and cinched waists.

By this point, fashion was really beginning to interest me. I was a huge fan of Coco Chanel as well as Christian Dior and I kept up with what all the fashionable figures of the day were wearing. I was more conscious of royalty and the upper classes than film stars, though, and the person who fascinated me most of all was Edith Sitwell, because she was so strange. She had an extraordinary hairdo – she shared a birthday with Queen Elizabeth I and wrote two books about her, so I think she shaved her hairline to give herself a similarly high forehead. She also wore extraordinary clothes. I suppose they were 'ethnic' clothes, which nobody wore then unless they were really ethnic (or a fan of the Pre-Raphaelites). Everybody else wore what I call 'ordinary' clothes – either poor, middle or upper class – so she really stood out from the crowd.

Working at Heelas was only ever going to be temporary, as I don't think shop work was quite what my mother had in mind for me. But riding was not well paid and I was pleased to be earning better money, as it meant I was able to give some to Mummy for housekeeping and have some left over for myself. I earned around £3 a week, which was fine in a time when bread was 4d, milk 5d and stamps tuppence halfpenny each – although I had to save up for bigger purchases like my Hercules bike, which cost £14 and 5 shillings.

I made friends with the other Heelas sales girls and we used to go to dances together. Going to a dance cost anything between 2 and 5 shillings. The theatre was a bit more – and a box at the Reading Palace was 24 shillings! Several of us got to know a group of officers from the Royal Electrical and Mechanical Engineers (REME) at Arborfield, who were good company. After we'd met them once, that was it, we were a little gang and all went out together. They invited us to the officers' mess dances, the Sandhurst balls, they came to Heelas's staff dances and others. The REME officers were away from their families and homes and we were only too pleased to have partners to go out with. A lot of them were married, but they weren't looking for affairs. They just wanted somebody to go out with and dance. It was all about the dance.

One night I wore a rather splendid but old-fashioned red crêpe dinner gown given to me by a friend of the

Linfoots. When I look at the photograph of that evening now, I realize that it was far too mature for me – what on earth was I thinking? It had a long pleated skirt, with three pleats on either side and a plain panel down the front, a sort of 'evening shirtwaister'. In the photo, my friend Yvonne looks terribly glamorous in a dress that practically comes off her shoulder, with me next to her in something that our head of department, Mrs Kay, might have worn. Perhaps it was the only thing I had to wear – and I certainly don't remember feeling awkward in it. Three of us girls had the temerity to get up and sing George Gershwin's 'S'Wonderful' that night!

I wasn't always so demurely attired. The same year, I made a Mickey Mouse outfit to wear to the Chelsea Arts Ball – shorts, a T-shirt and a mask. It was my love of dressing-up coming out again. I went to the ball with a very nice medical student called Sam. I had a lot of friends like Sam. Men were always after a partner to go out with because in those days you didn't go out by yourself, you always went with somebody. Most of the time there was a group of us, but you usually had a date; if you'd been out with somebody often enough, they might eventually get round to asking you to marry them. You hoped they wouldn't, because although they were quite nice to go out with, you didn't want to marry them. I brushed off several proposals. If you did it diplomatically, it wasn't too awkward and you could keep on going out with them. You just said something like 'I don't want to think about that at the moment'!

In July 1949, I went into work one day to find all the sales girls talking about a competition in the local *Reading Review* magazine. A photographer was looking for a cover girl. I was egged on to apply and to my surprise the photographer chose me for the job! The strangest thing was that, when we got talking, we discovered he and his wife had known my parents when they lived in Caversham in the 1930s and they had all been in the Reading Opera Society together.

'Gilbert Adams?' my mother said when I blurted out my exciting news to her that evening. 'Yes, I remember him. Wasn't his father a royal photographer?'

Mummy never forgot things like that and, indeed, Gilbert's father, Marcus, had taken some very famous pictures of the Queen Mother – when she was Duchess of York – and Princess Elizabeth before she became Queen and her sister Princess Margaret. His grandfather had also done the same job – they were a photographic dynasty.

Gilbert took a lot of photos of me and I learned how to behave in front of a camera. Photographers nowadays think it's fantastic, because so many models haven't been trained. Among other things, he taught me how to present my narrowest profile in a fashion shot, because clothes are deemed to look better on a thin person. Also – and this sounds very obvious now I'm writing it down – it is important to blink between shutter clicks.

Gilbert was experimenting with colour photography, which was still relatively new, so I was a good guinea pig for him. I also acted as his assistant when he went to photograph families and children in their own homes, which was his main profession. His father had a studio in Dover Street, London, and very occasionally I went there, but I never managed to get to any of the royal sittings.

A couple of months after I met Gilbert, I was exercising one of Charlie Budd's horses one morning when it took exception to something in the hedge and tipped me into a blackberry bush, breaking my collarbone. I managed to get myself and horse back to the stables and Charlie took me to hospital to be repaired – I had to be strapped up for three weeks! Gilbert was not best pleased with his new model, but it mended quickly and in the meantime he jolly well had to wait. When my collarbone healed it was a bit knobbly, but not noticeably – although my shoulders are not symmetrical, which makes tailoring tricky.

I was still working at Heelas and I think they had me in mind for a promotion to store buyer, because they sent me to a retail summer school at Wadham and Keble Colleges in Oxford for a week in the summer of 1949. I didn't think I would stay long enough to step up the ladder, but a week's course in Oxford was not to be missed. There were lectures and workshops by famous people in the rag trade, including Vernon Ely from Ely's of Wimbledon and James Laver the historian. There were museums to visit and dances to go to. All in work time! I took along my favourite pair of shoes – they were black with a two-inch heel and straps that criss-crossed the foot, which meant they stayed on nicely and were perfect for dancing. Recently I spotted someone wearing the very same style of shoe and wished I still had them! It was a marvellous week, especially since I got to know Oxford and some of its nightlife. We were supposed to be back in our colleges at ten every evening, but of course we weren't. I remember several breathless escapades climbing the walls to get back in after being locked out.

But it wasn't all adventures. There was also a very poignant moment in the chapel of Keble College, when I saw the original painting of *The Light of the World* by Holman Hunt. It was so much smaller than I had imagined, perhaps because I knew the life-size version that Hunt painted for St Paul's Cathedral towards the end of his life. I'm attached to it and always have been because I have a little reproduction of it, left to me by my cousin Adrian, who was killed in the war. I've never forgotten how kind Adrian was to me.

The *Reading Review* with me on the cover came out in January 1950 and soon afterwards Heelas staged a fashion show. The models – or mannequins, as they were known then – came down from London to take part. But when they arrived they realized that they were one person short. Somehow I was persuaded to fill the gap. I had never done anything like it before, and was rather apprehensive, but I managed to overcome my nerves. I like to think that I will try anything once – within reason, of course!

'That was actually rather fun,' I said to one of the models when it was over.

'I could see you were enjoying yourself,' she said. 'Look, why don't you train as a model and join our agency?'

I wouldn't have thought twice about it if she hadn't suggested it, but suddenly it seemed like a good idea. My mother thought it a much better option than working with dangerous horses, so in April I said goodbye to Heelas and joined Gaby Young's Agency in London the very next day.

Everything was changing for me. I had come of age and was no longer a horsey girl striding around in breeches (although I was still doing quite a bit of that, admittedly). I suppose I was finally grown up. I certainly felt it when Gilbert took me on his press pass to the 1950 Henley Regatta and we got photographed and had our pictures in all the papers. I had made a rather stunning outfit for the event – a white broderie anglaise dress, with a tight bodice and a big collar – and I wore it with a wide hat that I'd bought and trimmed. I had been to the Regatta before – with my parents, as guests of their friends – but this time I was the centre of attention, keeping the photographers busy.

It was also in 1950 that Charlie Budd took me on my first of many outings to Royal Ascot, another event where sport and fashion go hand-in-hand. Charlie took me to the dogs at Wembley, too, where we had dinner overlooking the track. It was wonderful. I was no longer on the periphery of things – excluded from the Pony Club, barred from the point-to-point, a stable girl in hand-me-downs, hoping for a horse. I was someone in my own right, with an exciting future ahead of me, and it all felt rather marvellous.

SIX

The Mink Stole

In 1950, if you were wearing mink, you'd arrived. Fur was highly desirable, a sign of status, especially sable, ermine, mink or fox. So I was delighted to land a job as a house model at L. Woolf, a highly reputable furriers in Grosvenor Street in Mayfair. The anti-fur movement was years away and at the time I didn't give it any thought, although I would now, of course.

On Gaby Young's advice I had taken a permanent modelling job. During my three-week course at her agency I'd learned how to walk down a catwalk, do a three-point turn and take off my coat or jacket whilst parading. There was also a lesson on how to get in and out of cars in a ladylike manner – knees firmly together. The other trainee models and I were taught to do our own hair and make-up and make the most of accessories like scarves, jewellery, handbags and gloves. It was all quite exciting to a country girl used to riding horses, but per-haps the most useful lesson would have been how to keep your job as well as your cool while fending off various employers' advances!

Once we had passed the eagle eye of Gaby Young,

herself an elegant model, we were sent to a photographer to have pictures taken for a 'card' with which we would go round to a list of photographers to see if we could get some work. As I did not have much financial back-up I was advised to take a permanent job so that I could build up some savings before going freelance. I could not at first rely on there being enough work to make ends meet, so I started casting about for something suitable.

My life had begun to revolve around London and I was commuting up from Wokingham on the train until I could find somewhere to live. Then my aunt Winnie, who lived in a block of flats in Oakley Street, Chelsea, found an empty one for me there. It was just two rooms – a bedroom and tiny sitting room with a sink and cooking facilities – pretty primitive by modern standards and, like others of its era, painted dark green and brown. Bathing and washing took place in the basement. Still, it was reassuring to have Auntie Winnie nearby and she was great fun, always out at concerts and the theatre and introducing me to her friends. Like her sister, Auntie Olive, she had never married, and her life was a social and cultural whirl.

My first job was as a house model at Landau and Diamond, a wholesale dress manufacturer in Margaret Street, where several other girls and I paraded samples of coats and dresses in front of retail buyers from nine to five. It was good fashion-business experience, but I also had to learn fast how to keep my rather keen employers at arm's length. They were far too friendly for my liking. Smiles accompanied by icy politeness seemed to do the trick. I know I lost a lot of acting and modelling jobs later on because I refused to go the casting-couch route.

After four months of this I was very glad when I landed the job at L. Woolf in Mayfair. This was an elite establishment and far more prestigious than Landau and Diamond. There was one photograph in the window and I felt so honoured to discover that now it was to be of me, wearing a fabulous wild mink fur stole and evening dress. It was a really nice job all round – and no unwanted advances. I was expected to show the furs, do some of the books, make the tea and generally look after the customers.

Fur had always been prized by the fashion world but it was difficult to work with unless you were a furrier. Then, in the early twentieth century, exciting advances in fur- and pelt-processing made it possible to render all types of fur softer, fluffier and easier to dye – making it irresistible to designers like Jeanne Lanvin and Paul Poiret in Paris.

Lanvin and Poiret introduced fur trims to their coats and jackets and soon started including fur stoles in their collections, as did Isadore Paquin. By the 1920s, most fashionable middle- and upper-class women were wearing full-length fur coats – and two out of three women in

England were wearing at least a fur trim, if not head-to-toe silver-blue mink. I have a photograph of Mummy from 1927 wearing a very chic fur-trimmed coat. And my grandmother Emily always had fur collars and cuffs on her winter coats, probably beaver or fox.

Life was colder without central heating, so fur was a practical option, but it was also a symbol of comfort and success. Women were often satirized as wanting a mink coat above all else, even a husband! Fur coats came in several brackets: the housewives' special, which might be rabbit, squirrel, mole or whatever else was going cheap; the middling range that included chinchilla and beaver; and luxury fur. If you had a car – although not many people did – you definitely had a long fur coat, as cars were exceptionally draughty in the 1920s. In my lifetime, society's view of fur has completely changed – I might say for the better!

I had fur-trimmed clothes as a toddler – rabbit, probably. Fox was the luxury fur of choice in the 1930s, but sales dropped off during the Great Depression and the Second World War because supply lines were patchy and people couldn't afford it. Demand rose again after the war, when mink took over from fox as the most desirable fur of all and became the ultimate in glamour and opulence, the height of conspicuous consumption. Royalty and the aristocracy wrapped themselves up in mink coats of various hues, and British and American movie stars, from Vivien Leigh to Marilyn Monroe, never stopped wearing them. Some people even wore mink earrings.

I modelled so many luxury furs at L. Woolf that it became a matter of course, but although I would probably have liked one at the time, I could never afford one! In the 1950s my coats were tweed or woollen cloth, or my New Look corduroy coat that started pale blue and ended up being dyed black. These days I have lots of faux fur, which is so good now that it's quite difficult to tell the difference. The main thing is that it's warm and cosy in the cold weather – I always like wearing my 'furry' coats. I've never owned a real fur coat and would never want one now. It's just awful to think of the beautiful animals being killed unacceptably for fashion and adornment. These days the faux alternatives are just fabulous – I wonder what L. Woolf would make of today's faux fur industry?

I got on well with my employers at Woolf's. Mrs Woolf was French and extremely glamorous. Her endeavours to smarten me up and turn me into a city girl began when I was taken to a designer house in Curzon Street and fitted with my own little black dress. It was a fairly plain style with a side drape, but effortlessly smart. Of course, the LBD had first been invented by Coco Chanel in the 1920s. Jean Patou also had a strong claim to its origins, but Chanel somehow won out. When American *Vogue* featured its first LBD in 1926, it was called

'Chanel's Ford' and *Vogue* said it would become 'a sort of uniform for all women of taste'. It was a simple, chic garment and so easy to wear – as it still is today.

Every week I was sent to Steiner's of London for a manicure, and to a hairdresser in Davis Street for my hairdo. My now shoulder-length auburn hair was washed and set in big rollers and dried under a hood that was lowered to eyebrow level. I'd sit under it for an hour, holding the controller in my hand in case it got too hot and had to be turned down, and eventually I would emerge from the salon with perfectly set, glossy hair – only to go and mess it up again at weekends when I'd take the big red double-decker bus from Victoria to Reading to go riding horses at home.

That first summer at Woolf's I discovered that August was a very dead month in London, so my friend Beryl Bateson and I went on a week's holiday to Padstow in Cornwall. Beryl and I had been neighbours for years in Wokingham, where we became best friends and remained best friends for life. We stayed with a Mrs Butterfield in a farmhouse at Great Crugmeer just outside the town, where the toilet arrangements were cause for much merriment and giggling. The facility was down the garden in its own little shed, where two people could sit side by side on highly polished mahogany seats on a raised dais like a throne. It was a great holiday and Mrs Butterfield was really kind, feeding us huge cooked breakfasts each morning before we went exploring in Padstow and all the surrounding beaches – Bedruthan Steps, Constantine Bay and many others. We took trips to Mevagissey and Fowey on the south coast and began to get to know and love Cornwall. I will never forget our trip to King Arthur's castle in Tintagel. The day started fine but rain soon set in and we got completely soaked. Beryl was wearing a new pair of maroon corduroy trousers and the dye began to run – she ended up with everything tinted pink, including her legs! It was such a job to clean up when we got back to the farm, but we had a big laugh in spite of it all.

Back in London, a friend of my mother's found me a large unfurnished flat in a mansion block in Queen's Club Gardens, Barons Court. Trevor was a property developer who did up houses and flats all over the south of England, which he would furnish and either let or sell on. I went with him on many a trip to explore new projects and he and his wife, Flo, would regularly take me to nightclubs in London – usually the Bagatelle in Mayfair – always making me drink a glass of milk before we went out to line my stomach before the champagne! They needn't have worried. Although I went to lots of dances and parties where the wine flowed, I only ever drank a little sherry or champagne. I was never keen on drinking – and I have never smoked.

The Bagatelle was *the* place to go in those days. Princess Elizabeth had made it famous in the 1940s by dancing in public there for the first time. It was run by the Trinidadian bandleader Edmundo Ros, who, later, was often invited to sing and play at Buckingham Palace. He had a wonderful voice. I saw lots of different acts there, including the Deep River Boys, an American gospel group who had performed with Fats Waller and Count Basie. Trevor was an excellent dancer and we had great fun. I never dreamt then that one day soon I would be dancing professionally in one of Edmundo Ros's clubs.

It was Christian Dior who coined the term 'cocktail dress' to refer to something you would wear in the early evening, but by this point we were beginning to wear our cocktail dresses to go to nightclubs and out dancing. I remember one dress particularly because I made it myself. It had a strapless bodice and flared skirt in grey taffeta, with a yellow sash over one shoulder, across the top and down one side over the hip. I also had a black taffeta skirt with a quilted embroidered border, which I wore with a lace top. A cocktail dress today is usually knee-length or above the knee, but in those days they were longer, at least calf-length if not just above the ankle.

One Friday evening around this time I was given a ticket for a film premiere in Leicester Square. To my delight, I sat behind Margaret Lockwood, the famous star best known for playing a highway robber in a hugely popular and rather racy film, *The Wicked Lady*. It was quite an occasion to be close to such glamour! I can't remember much about the film, just that it was in black and white, called *Highly Dangerous* and riven with Cold War fears and germ warfare. I suppose I was too busy trying to catch the occasional glimpse of Margaret Lockwood's profile to notice much else.

The next morning, Trevor and Flo took me up to Windermere in the Lake District in their Singer car. It had a front bench seat and so all three of us could sit together – no seat belts in those days – which was brilliant for seeing the country. It was a mammoth journey, but worth it for the far-reaching views over the lake from the hotel when we got there. The dinner was very good too. But there was altogether too much time spent in the car for someone active like me. It was a huge relief when we stopped at Doncaster on the way back to give us all a break and stretch our legs.

Now that I was only riding at weekends, I needed to find other ways of exercising, so I started doing evening ballet classes at the Mercury Theatre in Notting Hill Gate, dressed in the usual practice gear of leotard, tights, leg warmers and crossover cardigans. Marie Rambert had her company at the Mercury then – and if you didn't do the step or exercise right she would slap your legs. I was always on the sidelines, since I wasn't a trained dancer, but it led to an increasing interest in the world of ballet. The Ballet Rambert were amazing. I tried to see as many of their productions as I could, especially the ballets created by Antony Tudor.

At the other end of the cultural spectrum, I got to know and work with a photographer called Hugh White, who suggested I join a couple of shows he was putting on at Collins Music Hall in Islington, and later at the Walthamstow Palace, just for a week each. These were music hall revue shows, with different acts, dancers and showgirls, and I didn't have to do much except stand around in the background wearing sequins and being decorative. But it was a good introduction to theatre life and I got to know several of the professional dancers. Collins was a very old theatre with dressing rooms in the cellars, where it was quite usual to see rats scurrying about. It is now a branch of Waterstones.

My ballet education continued in the summer of 1951 – the year of the Festival of Britain – when Gilbert Adams asked if I would be his assistant while he took photographs of the Festival Ballet. Mainly he needed someone to carry his cameras and write down the names of the dancers as he photographed them. The Festival Ballet – now the English National Ballet – had been formed by Alicia Markova, Anton Dolin and Julian Braunsweg the previous year. It was wonderful to spend the next three weeks watching this fresh new company perform. I felt so privileged. They were appearing at the Stoll Theatre in Kingsway (now sadly gone and replaced by the rather stark and smaller Peacock Theatre, but at least there is still a theatre!).

We got to know the dancers and stage crew and would go out with them after the show, most often to the Buckstone Club in Piccadilly, where Gilbert was a member. Among our gang was the lighting director Jim Smith, a tall, good-looking, intelligent man who was to become an important part of my life, had I but known it then. Jim and I had a lot of fun at the Buckstone, which was run by Gerald Campion (who famously went on to play the title role in the popular BBC series *Billy Bunter of Greyfriars School*, even though he was decades too old for the role). The club was filled with famous actors – too many to list – but the one that sticks in my mind is the actor and playwright Hugh Burden, who asked me to marry him every time I walked through the door!

The highlight of these weeks, for me, was going on stage one evening as one of the crowd in Stravinsky's ballet *Petrouchka*. I don't know how I was persuaded to do it, but it turned out to be such a treat. The costume I was given was extremely tight because all the dancers were so much smaller than me, but I was determined to squeeze into it. And I succeeded, although I could hardly breathe. Firmly guided on either side by two expert dancers, I was thrilled to be making my first appearance in a professional ballet.

*

I don't know if there was something in the air, but visiting the Festival of Britain on the South Bank – and marvelling at the incredible Skylon and other futuristic attractions – inspired me to take a chance and leave Woolf's in the early autumn to go freelance as a model. The decision soon proved to be justified as, in the years that followed, I advertised a wide variety of products, including clothes, hats, cereals, beer, wine, gin, biscuits and bacon.

I am almost unrecognizable in one magazine advert I did, because of an unfortunate turn in the weather on my way to the studio. It began to snow furiously and by the time I arrived I was completely soaked. Of course, nobody did your hair for you – you just went as you were. So I posed for the photograph with a pint of beer in my hand and my naturally wavy hair plastered flat against my head. Fortunately, no one seemed to mind. It wasn't a shampoo advert. They just made the best of it.

Modelling in the 1950s was entirely different to how it is today. Models needed to supply their own accessories – jewellery, scarves, belts, shoes, gloves and underwear – and do their own hair and make-up. This involved carting around a huge holdall of everything that might be needed – in a time when suitcases didn't have wheels. Now you just go as you are and everything is done for you – although you do have to take the correct underwear.

Through Gaby Young's agency, I branched out a little further when I went with several other girls to do fashion shows at Beatty's of Wolverhampton, a smart department store. I also did one of the last shows for Marshall and Snelgrove in Cavendish Square in London. I'll always remember the lime-green taffeta halter-neck evening dress I wore, which was teamed with long black gloves with net frills. I felt that my broad shoulders were not best suited to a halter-neck and I have never been very keen on them since, but I loved the gloves and was allowed to keep them; my daughter Rose wore them years later.

I did a few fashion shows for Berkertex, one at Edwin Jones in Southampton – where I was staggered by the sight of the huge transatlantic liner RMS *Queen Mary* in dock – and four in different stores in Norwich. I enjoyed modelling Berkertex clothes – they had a subtle elegance about them and fitted me exceptionally well. Many were designed by the brilliant high-society couturier Norman Hartnell, who had a long-standing relationship with the company dating back to the government's utility project during the Second World War. Having designed Princess Elizabeth's wedding dress in 1947 – and so much more – Hartnell was one of the first big-name designers to design mass-produced, ready-to-wear clothing, while at the peak of his fame. It was a fantastic collaboration and he sprinkled glamour across the brand. I always felt good in Berkertex.

In August 1951, Beryl and I returned to Cornwall, this time to St Ives, a truly magical place. We spent a lot of our time on the beaches around the town. I wore a normal one-piece swimming costume for proper swimming and had several bikinis for sunbathing, as well as a wool bandeau top I'd knitted – nowadays known as a 'boob tube', although I don't imagine people knit their own any more. We all wore such things on the beach – and I wore the boob tube with a skirt or shorts around the town.

Gilbert Adams and his family always holidayed there and Gilbert introduced us to many of his artist friends, including Sven Berlin, the sculptor, who lived at Cripplesease with Juanita, his bohemian wife, children and goats. We also met Gilbert's friend Alec Brooke, who lived in a house on the edge of the cliffs at Zennor, overlooking the Atlantic. He was experimenting with 'polarized light' and Gilbert was very interested. Afterwards we visited the Tinners Arms and drank real draught cider, which was lovely and smooth, but had a lethal effect if you were not careful! We went to the Lizard, Mousehole, Penzance and Lamorna, sometimes sketching, sometimes just sitting in the Copper Kettle in St Ives, drinking coffee, always with friends. Gilbert took endless photographs, a lot of them of me! Our fortnight passed far too quickly.

At the end of the year, I was booked to do a New Year's Eve show at the Cumberland Hotel in Marble Arch. We models were brought in to provide some glamour back-up for Buddy Bradley's troupe of dancers.

People on the go and on the grow

are strong for the Sunshine Breakfast

Why? It's simple. Kellogg's Corn Flakes give you the full strength and all the nourishment of rich grain, ripened in the strong sunshine of a long hot summer. What's more, they're fortified with important vitamins. (Kellogg's add them specially.)

Then there's the famous Kellogg's taste. The crisp golden taste that no one has ever been able to match. That's why people on the go and on the grow (people like you) have made Kellogg's Corn Flakes the world's number one breakfast.

Kellogg's CORN FLAKES *Crispest Nourishment under the Sun*

17. One of my first commercials for Kellogg's, shot in 1965.
My riding skills came in handy!

18. One of my most successful promotional photos from the 1960s.

19. One for the portfolio – I made the suit.

20. A great 1970s Berkertex outfit. This photo was displayed in the window of the Swan & Edgar store in Piccadilly, London.

21. Our 25th wedding anniversary, 1979, with Rose, Claire and Mark. The dress is another of my own creations.

22. I made this 1930s-style suit on a City & Guilds course in the 1980s.

23. The Dannimac years of the 1980s.

24. Another City & Guilds creation in purple,
my favourite colour. I still wear this dress to this day.

25. The mother of the bride. A dress I made for
Claire and Dick's wedding in 1989.

26. Keeping up with my ballet stretches in a
Saga magazine shoot in 2002.

Buddy was famous for choreographing the Rodgers and Hart musical *Evergreen*, which became a 1930s film with Jessie Matthews. An African American who had settled in England, he was also the first black dancer to choreograph a West End show – and he was a lovely, charming man.

After the Cumberland show, he came up to me and said, 'Would you like to come up to my school? I think you would make a good dancer.'

Well, that was interesting! The full extent of my dancing experience was taking a few classes at the Mercury Theatre, but I went anyway and spent an intensive week trying all his classes, including ballet, modern, tap and Spanish dancing. I was pretty stiff at the end of it, but being naturally flexible, I managed, and subsequently Buddy offered me a place at the school, paying half price. When I explained that it was all very well, but I had to earn my living, he said, 'Just come to whichever classes you can, then.'

So at the ripe old age of twenty-three I started to train as a dancer. I persevered and went to classes whenever I could. And I loved every minute, although my ballet teacher – Hilda Lumley of the International Ballet – was not best pleased that I was still going hunting and riding at the weekends, as riding and ballet are conflicting disciplines. Tap was the most difficult class for me, especially as we did our routines to Buddy's intricate American rhythms. Once, when it came to our solo spot in the class, I actually did it right! Everyone clapped and I felt a huge sense of achievement. One of my other teachers was Liz Shelley, Buddy's leading lady, a very exotic-looking girl with bright orange hair. Then there was Ann Emery, who had tremendous patience with me. I owe a lot of my success in the dance world to her. The sister of the late comedian and actor Dick Emery, Ann was a brilliant soubrette in her own right and had done many shows and pantomimes. Her final role was Grandma in the West End show *Billy Elliot*, which she played for many years (with a couple of interludes for other roles) until she retired in 2014.

Eventually, after much hard work, I became a reasonably good dancer. I continued classes and modelling – and later in the year I spent a couple of weeks holding the fort at the *Country Gentleman's Magazine* for my friend Julienne, while she was on holiday. I knew Julienne through Beryl Bateson. They had met at secretarial college and the three of us were firm friends. The *Country Gentleman's Magazine* offices were just off Piccadilly and I enjoyed my time there; although I did lots of filing and typing letters, I also helped design the cover for the next issue. However, it firmed my resolve never to do a sitting-down, nine-to-five job – my restless spirit found it far too restricting to be confined to a seat in an office.

I much preferred dancing. Buddy had a small troupe

of dancers who did TV and nightclub shows and I appeared several times in a show called *Café Continental* at Lime Grove – the main BBC studio at that time. My friend Christine and I had to dress as flunkeys and open the doors to a TV nightclub, the 'Café Continental'. The show was compered by Hélène Cordet, the French-born Greek actress and cabaret star who was famous for her friendship with the Duke of Edinburgh, and it featured many famous stars of the time. Once we had opened the doors, Christine and I would stand in the wings and watch the acts. In one show we saw the wonderful Josephine Baker, who really was completely fabulous in every way. We also saw Jacques Tati, the French mime artist and star of *Monsieur Hulot's Holiday*, who did a sketch in which he attempted to lead a reluctant, imaginary horse out of a stable. We had a job not to laugh out loud, it was so hilarious.

When I wasn't doing classes or dancing, I often modelled for students at the Camera Club in the evenings. The previous summer, in St Ives again, Gilbert had suggested that I phone the artist and sculptor Barbara Hepworth to see if she wanted a model while we were all down there. Knowing that she was a well-known sculptor, I nervously picked up the phone to see if she needed me. She liked drawing dancers' bodies, so I posed for her at her studio in Trewyn quite a few times then and in later years, although I never got to know her very well because she never said very much. She drew me in red and blue chalks and I felt quite comfortable posing in the nude, quite at ease in my body. It was just another way of earning some holiday money and I didn't worry about it in any way, as I was an experienced life model by now after all! To augment my income while I was in St Ives, I posed for other artists and also worked in the Picnic Box, a sandwich bar on Westcotts Quay. This was the best of jobs, as the hours fitted in with spending time on the beach and modelling. In those days the summers always seemed to be hot and sunny and we did a lot of swimming, surfing and sunbathing. I just loved being on the beach, never giving a thought to the harmful effects of the sun as we fried ourselves with sun oil to get a good tan.

We went to the Minack Theatre, situated outdoors on the edge of the cliffs. One performance was *Arthur of Britain*; a 'midnight matinee'. With the sea and sky as background it was truly amazing. There were only rough narrow paths down to the stone seats and climbing down clutching a necessary cushion was pretty tricky in the dark. I've still got a scar where I grazed my knee on a rock that night! All very different now, of course, with carefully designed ramping.

I also went along to the St Ives School of Art and modelled for life classes there. Leonard Fuller was head of the school then, and he did a painting of me that I acquired some years later. I also modelled for Malcolm

Haylett, who did a painting of me for a John Bull cover, and for William Redgrave and Hymen Segal, who had studios near each other.

Back in London, as well as modelling at the Camera Club, I posed as a figure model at the Slade School of Art and at art schools in Chelsea and further afield in Reading, just a short train ride away. I also worked for another sculptor, Mary Audsley, in Kensington – endlessly. She always seemed to take such a long time to do anything! I did fifty-one sittings for one particular piece.

At the Slade, the first two poses were always forty-five minutes each, standing or sitting, then several short fifteen-minute poses for the rest of the day. Fortunately, I was able to keep still – otherwise I would have been out of a job. William Coldstream was the principal then and he decided he wanted to paint me, so, on and off for about eighteen months, after working with the students I would go to his studio. Luckily, he wanted me in a reclining pose.

He didn't speak much and never let me see the painting, even when he had nearly finished it. But I immediately recognized it when I went along to the Coldstream retrospective at the Tate in 1987 – I couldn't forget that pose after spending so long in one position. But to my surprise – and slight indignation – the model was named as someone else, which I soon put right with the organizer of the exhibition. She made it up to me with a nice lunch, a free catalogue and a marvellous visit to the South Bank collection, where Sir William's paintings are deposited.

Around the time I was modelling for art students, in the summer of 1953, I started to think that it might be nice to settle down. I was about to turn twenty-five and that seemed like a good age to marry and start a family. But with whom? I wasn't impressed by a lot of the men I knew – there were so many wolves out there! None of my friendships ever seemed to become serious and I didn't find myself falling in love.

Then one night I brought on the basket of castanets for the Spanish dancers in a big charity one-night-only show, *Merely Players*, at the Theatre Royal, Drury Lane – and bumped into Jim Smith, who had been the lighting director at the Festival Ballet when I was assisting Gilbert Adams. That Sunday night he was stage manager, and during the week he was working at Drury Lane on *The King and I*. As it happened, I did like Jim. He was very good-looking and not in the least bit wolfish. Tall – over six foot – slim and handsome, he had a kind face and a manner that put me at ease and made me feel relaxed. We were already good friends and had seen each other quite a few times since our nights out at the Buckstone – we'd met at various theatre events, and for quick snacks here and there between classes and rehearsals, and at other people's parties, too. That night we said hello and went our separate ways, but I remember thinking how much I liked him.

In September 1953, Jim went through his list of girl-friends to see if one of them was available to take to the first night of the Walter Gore Ballet. Luckily, I was free! And that was the evening we decided we would end up together. After the ballet we went for a drink at the Buckstone Club, very pleased with ourselves and making plans long into the night. How life can change in a moment! We had proved that we got on well together and had much in common in lots of areas – a love of theatre, dance, art and London and the same circle of friends. We had been friends for two years and he had always been gentlemanly and respectful, while other men had been keen to pressurize me for their own ends, rather than think of me and what I wanted. And the timing was just right. We were both looking to settle down and felt that we had found the right partner to do that with. Over time, I was to discover we had even more in common than I'd thought, as he had the same love of history and academia as my father – rather unexpected in a theatre person!

Jim had a flat at the top of Cardinal Cap House, on the Thames at Bankside. The entrance had an impressive black-and-white tiled floor and a beautiful ceiling painted by the seventeenth-century decorative painter James Thornhill. It had been owned previously by a relation of

Axel Munthe, the author of *The Story of San Michele*, and legend has it that Christopher Wren lived there while he was building St Paul's Cathedral, on the opposite bank. I remember going for tea there and having tinned peaches and cream looking over the river at St Paul's. Tinned fruit was such a treat in those days.

Buddy's dancers were doing a season at the Coconut Grove in Regent Street, so I was juggling my modelling during the day and dancing at night. Working as a night-club dancer in the 1950s was very different from anything that you might imagine from the same job description today, of course. Edmundo Ros was running the club and he was very particular. Even though we dancers were going to change into our costumes as soon as we arrived, we had to wear cocktail frocks to walk through the club to our dressing rooms! We used to grumble at the time, but with dress standards having relaxed so far nowadays, I quite like the idea.

One night Jim came to watch the show and Edmundo wouldn't let him in because he was wearing a pullover under his jacket, rather than a waistcoat. A big row ensued, which I witnessed first-hand as I had arrived with Jim. It was quite a serious confrontation; Edmundo was not prepared to relax his dress code for anyone and Jim wasn't going to back down. In the end, Jim had to leave, as he would rather not go in than take off his pullover.

I was so cross with them both, and so very embarrassed. Oh, for being surrounded by strong, immovable men!

Buddy's show at the Coconut Grove didn't involve the type of high-kicking routines that the Tiller and Bluebell Girls made famous. Instead, it was choreographed as a series of numbers known as 'story ballets', using ballet, tap and modern dance to describe a narrative, depending on the number. I did several routines: in 'Lonesome Road', I was a 'street walker' wearing a red satin slit skirt, black stockings and suspender belt and a tiny black hat; and in 'Carnival', I wore a bra top and shorts covered in artificial flowers. Among the other numbers were 'Leave Us Leap', 'Should I?', 'Blue Moon' and 'Smoochie'.

Loving clothes as I did, I helped sew many of the costumes. In fact, I think I got my place in Buddy's company mainly because I was a costume maker who 'could dance a little'! Liz, our leading lady, always wore elaborate outfits with sequins and feathers, but I tended to work on the character costumes. We wore thick ballet tights or fishnets when necessary, or leg make-up if it was called for – and heavy panstick foundation with lots of black eyeliner and mascara.

Midway through December, I went on my first dancing tour with Buddy's company to Belgium. We were booked to perform at the Ancienne Belgique Music Halls in Antwerp and Brussels – a week in each, twice, which meant lots of packing and unpacking! It was my first time out of England and very exciting – it was quite a treat for us all, as no one had travelled much since the war. But first we had to get through the crossing from Dover to Ostend, which was terrible. In fact, it was so rough that those of us who decided it would be less sick-making to be on deck, in the fresh air, were roped into a space amidships, so that we couldn't fall overboard.

I was very glad when we docked. We went by coach to our hotel, which was homely and comfortable, and then on to the Ancienne Belgique to sort out rehearsals and our place in the programme. The stage had huge red velvet curtains and the audience sat on red velvet chairs at little round tables, drinking and eating while they watched the show. Those plush red drapes, the stage, brass rails and steps were still there when I went back nearly fifty years later, in 2001, while I was in Antwerp doing a commercial for an insurance company. But by then the building had been taken over by an American clothing firm and there were rails of clothes in place of the seats – although it is a listed building and is apparently still used occasionally for charity performances.

Some of the other acts were practising when we arrived that first time, and we went on to make friends with all kinds of performers – singers, dancers, acrobats and musicians. There was a lovely sense of camaraderie and at one point I found myself trying to ride a unicycle. The highlight for us all was meeting the famous pop singer Jean Vallon. He was tall, blond, good-looking and so, so charming and friendly. Although he didn't have much English, where there is a will there is a way, and we just about managed to communicate. Antwerp looked very enticing at that time of year, with festive lights and decorations everywhere. We spent Christmas Day at the hotel and a great time they gave us.

Then it was on to the Ancienne Belgique in Brussels, which is still a working theatre today. We spent our spare time looking at all the shops and beautiful buildings – especially the big square in Brussels – and trying to speak French and Walloon, too. You were only allowed to take £30 out of the country then, but we made the most of it. Altogether it was a wonderful trip, despite the ferociously bumpy crossing back to Dover.

By the start of 1954 I felt that at last I was making headway as both a model and a dancer. However, after one last spectacular flourish, it was all set to come to an end. Jim and I became engaged in January and although we didn't have a firm wedding date in mind, circumstances rather quickly caught up with us. Discovering that I was pregnant at the end of April, we had to make fast plans, as it was not the done thing to have a child out of wedlock. For the time being, at least, I would focus on becoming – and being – Mrs Jim Smith, wife and soon-to-be mother. I didn't think I would work much again. After all, this was the 1950s!

SEVEN

Antique Lace Veil

There were two key styles of wedding dress in the early 1950s. The first was the traditional, full-length gown, often made of thick cream satin, studded with pearls and worn with a tiara, which could be a rather grand and formal affair. The second was a shorter, lighter, youthful, New Look-influenced dress that 'tipped the ankles' and was created using sheer fabrics like chiffon and lace. This had a bit more fizz to it.

I went for the modern silhouette. My dress was lace and georgette with long sleeves, a small waist and a full crinoline skirt made of tiers of gathered white silk. The skirt was ankle-length, with a diaphanous outer layer that showed off my ankles and strappy silver sandals. My veil couldn't have been more traditional, being the ornate 1862 Brussels cream lace veil that my mother had worn at her wedding in 1919, and yet it went very well with the dress. I wore minimal jewellery – just a pair of diamanté Dior earrings that Auntie Winifred gave me as a wedding present.

I left all the arrangements to my mother and mother-in-law, Myra, while I went off on my 'spectacular flourish', a two-month-long European dancing tour with Buddy Bradley's company, arriving home just four days before I got married. The idea of a prima donna bride who needs every last detail to be perfect on her wedding day was utterly foreign to me – and to my friends. We didn't get worked up about things like that. In those days, mothers organized weddings – for better or for worse.

The trip to Europe was quite an adventure. We went by boat and train, a seemingly never-ending journey delayed by engine trouble and bureaucratic hold-ups. There was a lot of waiting around at the Spanish border town of Irun, where we sat and watched donkeys carrying their loads through the streets, and when we eventually arrived in Madrid at the beginning of May there was a heatwave. But none of us cared a jot. It was so exciting to be in Spain's capital city for a whole month, with plenty of time for sightseeing.

By day, we explored the Prado and the beautiful parks, visited the Palacio Real, went to a bullfight and dropped into the cafes and bars playing flamenco music. We often had to run the gauntlet of the Spanish men calling out '*Guapa!*', meaning gorgeous or beautiful, as we walked along the streets. We sampled all kinds of unfamiliar food, from Spanish omelette to paella, all very appetizing. A friend of mine from St Ives was working in Madrid and I met up with him for lunch one day at the

Velázquez Club, where we had strawberries in wine, which I didn't like but ate to be polite!

By night, we danced at the Casablanca nightclub, where we actually did a Spanish number as part of our show. The audience thought it was wonderful, but I'm not so sure what they made of some of our costumes. Since the skimpier outfits – which were really nothing more than bikinis – did not meet strict Spanish dress codes, we had to modify them with what came to be known as our 'Spanish vests'. These were ordinary vests that we dyed in tea to make them flesh-coloured, then cut up and sewed between the tops and bottoms of our costumes. There was no stretch material or anything in those days, so we probably had wrinkly midriffs, but at least we were 'decent'!

After Madrid, we headed to Rome, again by train, overnight. It was an absolutely ghastly journey in carriages reeking of garlic and body odour. There was nowhere to sleep properly and we were exhausted by the time we at last arrived. Luckily, our digs were comfortable and fairly near the Via Veneto, where we were performing at La Rupe Tarpea, a nightclub in an underground grotto. We spent two weeks there and another two at the Belvedere della Rosa, a beautiful outdoor club slightly further out of the city, near the Appian Way, where one night the Aga Khan came to see the show.

We had a lot of fun and explored all the amazing sights

that Rome has to offer. I threw my coins in the Trevi Fountain, but although I have been to other parts of Italy since, I have not, so far, returned to Rome. Then, before I knew it, it was time to head home to get married. I barely slept on the journey back. I'd had two thrilling months in Europe and now there was even more excitement ahead of me.

Everything was prepared when I arrived home. All that I had been required to do was a little shopping while I was away. So I'd browsed Madrid's boutiques at every opportunity and eventually found my 'going away' suit – a beautiful, washable, wrap-over white jacket and skirt made of thick embossed cotton. (I still have it today, although I've since tailored the jacket to wear to Ascot and other such places.) In Rome I came across a pink top to wear under the jacket, as well as a perfect pair of black leather Italian sandals. How cosmopolitan I was becoming!

Earlier in the year, just after we had set the date of the wedding, Mummy and I had been wondering about what I should wear on the day. Buddy's company were rehearsing a new show at the Coconut Grove and I was rushed off my feet, so I was worried that I wouldn't have time to go to dress fittings. I certainly didn't have the time or expertise to make my own wedding dress. I could sew, but I wasn't that good. Later on, when I became more proficient, I did make a couple of wedding dresses for friends, but I wouldn't have been able to embark on one before I was married.

That's when we came across a dress hire service in a catalogue. 'What a really good idea!' Mummy said. 'Since you're going to be so busy dancing and modelling in the coming months, why don't we hire your wedding dress?'

'Yes, let's,' I said, feeling relieved. It was one less thing to fit into my schedule.

The dress had arrived in the post by the time I got back from Rome – and it was perfect. I'm easy to fit, luckily. So there was nothing really for me to do during the next few days apart from enjoy spending time with my parents and keep my fingers crossed for good weather.

The sixth of July 1954 turned out to be a warm, sunny day. Our family home was now in Bexhill, East Sussex, where my parents had lived since May 1952, and Jim and I got married at the Church of St Peter in the old town and had the reception in my parents' garden. As we made our way to the church, my father took my hand and said, 'I wish you all the happiness in the world, darling. I hope you and Jim will be every bit as contented in your marriage as Mummy and I have been for all these years.'

It was a very sweet thing to say, at just the right moment. I wanted to tell him how grateful I was to have been brought up in a happy, harmonious home without any tension or arguments. Having seen a bit of the world and talked to friends about their experience of childhood, I knew how lucky I was. What I probably didn't quite realize then was that my positive outlook and practical approach to life were almost entirely due to my upbringing. I owed my parents everything and I loved them dearly.

It wasn't a big wedding – we had around sixty guests and a lot of them were older relations and friends invited by my mother – but all the people I loved best were there, so I had a very happy time. My best friend, Beryl Bateson, was my bridesmaid. She wore a spotted summer dress with cap sleeves, a full skirt and a shaped neckline that mirrored the neckline of my dress. Some of my dancing friends from Buddy's company came along, as well as the cast of *The King And I*.

The mothers' outfits were very different, but they both looked stunning and stylish in their way. Mummy was in a brown lace dress, a sable fur, brown gloves and sandals, offset by her big cream hat and cream handbag. Myra, Jim's mother, wore a tailored grey suit, black accessories and a tiny hat. All the men were in the usual morning dress with white carnation buttonholes. The other guests wore normal 'wedding' or 'best' clothes – nothing outrageous. Everyone looked sort of similar in those days, young and old. All the women wore hats and gloves.

It wasn't a long drawn-out affair like people have

now. After a delicious buffet tea, champagne and a slice of the three-tiered wedding cake, Jim and I went off quite early, at about six. That night, we stayed at a hotel near the airport; the following day we flew to Nice and travelled on to Monte Carlo, where we spent our honeymoon. Jim's mother paid for our flights, which was jolly good of her. It was very unusual to fly anywhere then.

We stayed at a little hotel on the harbour that Jim knew – he had been in Monte Carlo with the Festival Ballet a couple of years before and knew his way around, so he cleverly booked a room overlooking the promenade. (It's gone now, sadly – they've altered the front and it's all high-rise apartments and hotels.) We had a blissful week exploring Monte Carlo and the French Riviera and I felt very happy to be married to Jim. We went to Menton one day, and to Nice, and spent a few scorching days on the beach. We didn't dress up much – mostly I wore my pretty Horrockses summer dresses. One had oranges and lemons all over it and another had a pattern in several shades of blue, turquoise and white – Jim liked this one in particular. Men always love it when you put on something blue, in my experience.

It was in Menton that we saw Maurice Chevalier, the French actor and cabaret singer, and had a drink with him after his show. Jim had worked with him in London a few years before and they were friends; I found him charming, as expected. He was already a well-known film star, but he was set to become even more famous a few years later when he sang 'Thank Heaven For Little Girls' in *Gigi*.

Another day we made our way up to La Turbie above Monte Carlo to visit Jim's friend David Lichine, a ballet dancer and choreographer who had danced with the Ballets Russes and worked in Hollywood. Jim had ballet friends everywhere. In the months before we were married, he had moved out of his flat on the river and was living with the Beriosoffs in Hans Crescent, Knightsbridge: Nickolai Beriosoff was a Lithuanian dancer and choreographer; his wife, Lilene, made costumes for the theatre; and his daughter, Svetlana Beriosova, was a principal ballerina with the Royal Ballet at Covent Garden. They were a warm, affectionate family with lots of friends coming and going and they made me very welcome.

Jim's close connection with ballet came partly through his mother, who had been spotted at ballet school at the age of seven and went on to dance with the company formed by Mikhail Mordkin and Anna Pavlova. She had started life as Blanche Lillian James and was known variously as 'Little Jamie' and 'Blanchetta' during her career, but I always knew her as 'Myra', which is Russian for 'darling'. She wasn't dancing by the time I met her, but she was teaching ballet from her studio at home in Richmond. I think she gave up performing when she married Jim's father, Sidney Smith, who worked for the Foreign

Office until he died in 1944 – but she had been well known in her day, touring all over Europe and America with the company Mordkin founded after he and Pavlova had a furious row and went their separate ways.

Jim had a similar background to mine, despite having an ex-ballerina for a mother. In fact, his upbringing was probably even more conservative, because he spent a lot of his childhood with his grandmother while his parents were posted abroad. He was four years older than I was, which made a crucial difference in the era we grew up in, as it meant he could enlist in the RAF during the war – although I think he still had to lie about his age. After leaving St Paul's Boys' School, he joined the Air Force, like his father before him. He passed his pilot's licence in a Tiger Moth and spent most of the war in South Africa training other soldiers to fly.

He did all sorts of things to earn money when the war finished. He drove a tram and he even went down a coal mine for a short spell – people were needed to do essential jobs after the war because so many had been killed. He started his career in the theatre stoking the boiler at the Lindsey Theatre in Notting Hill Gate and from there he worked his way up. He had a turn on the stage but didn't fancy it and eventually became a lighting director and stage manager, going on to work at the Theatre Royal, Drury Lane, with Jack Walters.

He had done an awful lot in the theatre before I met

him, working for the Festival Ballet and other ballet companies, several variety shows, Maurice Chevalier, George Robey and the Indian dancer Mrinalini Sarabhai. He knew what was what when it came to lighting and stage managing, but he was a quiet, unassuming man, much like my father, so nobody could believe he was such a whizz in the theatre.

After we returned from our honeymoon, we decided to move into my flat in Queen's Club Gardens, as it was spacious and convenient for the theatre. It was on the second floor, right on the corner of the block, so our sitting room had almost turret-like proportions. We had two bedrooms, a sitting room, kitchen and bathroom and there were public gardens with tennis courts in the middle of the block.

The flat lacked everything but the most basic furniture when I moved in. Since I had very little money, I sewed my own curtains and collected orange boxes from the fruit market, turned them on end and covered them with material to make bedside tables and suchlike. It was a great way of making do – and all my friends did the same. As time went on, I supplemented my meagre furniture with bits and pieces from the second-hand shops in the nearby North End Road and elsewhere. I wasn't into a particular style – I just went for what I could find that would suit my needs, all very cheap and cheerful. Already in the flat was the most memorable piece from those days, which I still have and cannot better – a kitchen table with legs that unscrewed, making it very transportable. It has resided in all our kitchens ever since!

I was pleased that my work wasn't affected when I first became pregnant with our son, Mark, as I wasn't ready to sit around knitting bonnets and booties. I was really lucky – being tall, I didn't show until the last month, when I started to look a bit thick round the waist. I didn't have to buy anything special, or adjust my existing clothes. I remember I had a tartan skirt that fitted me throughout, a couple of loose dresses and a creamy white duffel coat. It amuses me to watch programmes like *Call the Midwife*, where they all look like they've got footballs in their stomachs, as I was never like that. I did a fashion show for Berkertex at four months and a photo shoot for Walter Bird five months into the pregnancy – and I was still going to dance classes until I was seven months pregnant. I was trotting about doing all kinds of things and felt very well throughout, so I didn't give it a second thought.

In the lead-up to Christmas, I helped Lilene Beriosova sew costumes for the Howard and Wyndham panto-mimes, which were performed at several of the big theatres in London, like the Palace and the Palladium. Lilene was very good at costumes and I learned a lot from her. She worked on several productions at once and I used to go to her flat and make all sorts of things. Sometimes I took my work home with me and one week I made part of a 'holly' costume, with green velvet and satin leaves and ping-pong balls painted red for the berries. I had to hang them up on a string in the bathroom to dry and they gave Jim quite a shock when he came home that evening!

Mark was born the following January 1955 at Parson's Green Nursing Home, just as the curtain went up at Drury Lane, which meant that Jim did not see him until the next morning. In those days fathers did not participate at the birth as they do today. When we came home from the clinic, my godmother, Winifred Bentall, came to help, which was wonderful, as she was a children's nurse. She moved in with us for a few weeks and told me what to do – or did it herself – and soon I was more than capable of managing on my own.

I enjoyed staying at home and being a mother. It was hard work, but I never minded. Without a washing machine, nappies had to be soaked in a bucket and then washed and put to dry on a wooden rack in front of the fire. Fortunately, Mummy had taught me to cook, so I could manage that quite well. I made friends with a mother on the next landing who had a boy of about six and she helped me out with local shopping and occasional babysitting. Eventually, they had to move and, as her son had grown too big for his wooden rocking horse, she passed it on to Mark. It was a very thoughtful gesture and much appreciated, and all the grandchildren have played with him over the years.

When he was tiny, I dressed Mark in little white dresses and knickers. In those days, everyone dressed their newborn babies in white. There were no ultrasound scans, so you didn't know in advance whether you were going to have a boy or a girl, and white was a neutral colour. Anyway, the idea of gender colour coding – of 'blue for a boy' and 'pink for a girl' – was still relatively new, or at least it hadn't caught on like it has today. When it was introduced as a marketing ploy after the First World War, it was pink or red for a boy – because these were considered to be robust colours – while blue was deemed a suitably delicate colour for girls. Someone else decided it should be pink for blondes and blue for brunettes; then it was pink for brown-eyed children and blue to match blue eyes. So it was all a bit of a confusion. What's more, before we all had washing machines, it was more effective to boil wash and bleach white clothes. Practicality won the day.

To me all that mattered was making sure that Mark was clean and warm enough. I was lucky, as I was given a lot of baby outfits in a variety of colours, many of them handmade or knitted, and I knitted things myself as well. Everyone was delighted to be able to contribute and I don't remember buying anything.

*

In the summer of 1955, Jim decided he'd like to join the new commercial television station, ATV. He thought that a settled job with a regular salary would be better suited to married life with a young family than working in the theatre. He applied and was accepted and that September was part of the first broadcast by a commercial company. He worked on a great many different types of programmes – outside broadcasts, variety, advertising 'magazines' and all sorts of light entertainment – but is best remembered for doing Val Parnell's *Sunday Night at the London Palladium*, right from the very first show. In fact, he devised all the games for 'Beat the Clock' – a series of light-hearted challenges that members of the audience had to complete in a certain time, in a spot in the middle of the programme. This was quite something, as *Sunday Night at the London Palladium* soon became iconic television. One episode had an audience of 20 million!

Every Friday Jim went to the Palladium for rehearsals and every Sunday for the show. He did this for twelve years! Luckily, having been in the business too, I understood irregular hours. Sometimes I would go and watch the show – babysitters permitting – and as Mark grew up he loved to spot the back of Jim's head and his headphones on our black-and-white television screen.

The papers and magazines talked endlessly about *Sunday Night at the London Palladium*, and occasionally

Jim was interviewed. In an article for *Men Only* magazine about 'Beat the Clock', a writer named Gordon Glover memorably described him as, 'the gentle Torquemada of the Palladium Show'. Jim and I thought it was a rather funny comparison.

'Jim Smith himself is quite unfunny,' Glover also wrote. 'What would you expect – surely a cackling joker with pocketfuls of exploding cigars, finger-snapping matchboxes, rubber pencils and beetles for the beer? Dead wrong. Mr Smith, at 37, looks the kind of pleasant, serious-minded sort of chap you might find upon a housing committee.' A *housing committee*? This we found even funnier, as it was so unlikely!

Over the years, Jim worked with lots of different compères, among them Tommy Trinder, Robert Morley, Jim Dale, Roy Castle and Bruce Forsyth. All sorts of amazing acts appeared on the show, including Judy Garland, Sammy Davis Junior, Johnnie Ray, Shirley Bassey, Harry Secombe, Alfred Marks, Norman Wisdom, Ken Dodd, Bob Hope and even, eventually, the Rolling Stones – Jim used to like Mick Jagger's father very much. Jim kept a book with everybody's autographs in it. It was a fascinating treasure, documenting a slice of unforgettable television history.

As for me, I never tired of being a housewife and mother. You read about housewives in the 1950s feeling bored, sad and repressed, but I had none of that, thankfully. We were very social and were always out – we had a lot of showbiz friends and I had plenty of babysitters. We often went to the theatre, and we jolly well dressed up to go, too! That's something I grumble about nowadays – people don't dress up at all when they go to the theatre.

We would always be given tickets to shows at Drury Lane or the Palladium, which was wonderful. I remember one amazing Sunday night at the Palladium when there was a major power cut and Bruce Forsyth and Norman Wisdom had to ad lib the whole show. I see in my diary that the next day I went to see *Plain and Fancy* at Drury Lane. It was, oddly, a musical about an Amish community in America, but I rather enjoyed it. Later, I was lucky enough to see the original London productions of *My Fair Lady* and *West Side Story*, both of which I loved. During the 1950s I fell in love not only with Jim but with the musical shows of the time. I adored the romantic tales, the spectacle, the singing and dancing and, of course, the wonderful costumes. I still like to go to the theatre whenever I can.

In June 1958, Jim, Mark and I moved out of London to Haslemere in Surrey. We went with ATV's blessing – they said they would be building new studios at Vauxhall, which would be very convenient for commuting from Surrey. It seemed the perfect location for both country life and easy access to London, and my parents lived only about forty minutes away from Haslemere, making it even more suitable.

My mother looked after three-year-old Mark while we moved and settled in. We hired a removal van and Jim and I sat with the driver on the front bench seat as we made our way to our new home with our few possessions on board, stopping at a cafe for sausages and mash en route. Since we didn't have much stuff, we were soon unpacked! The house was a 1930s chalet bungalow just outside the town, overlooking the River Wey and National Trust woods on the far side. Jim bought a bicycle to get him to Haslemere station and back every day, and we were very excited to have our own home at last.

However, soon after we had settled in, Jim came home with terrible news. 'ATV have decided to put the new studios in Borehamwood!' he told me glumly. It was very frustrating – Borehamwood, being north of the Thames, was almost as inconvenient as it could get. There was no M25 then and the train links were hopeless, so it meant a horrible journey by road into London and out the other side.

'Are we going to have to move again?' I asked, aghast.

'Not yet, but we won't be here for good, as we'd hoped,' he said, putting a comforting arm round me. He was right that it didn't matter too much to begin with, as he was doing outside broadcasts, but later on when he became Head Floor Manager and was based at the studios, it had a huge impact on our lives.

Until then, we just got on with things and enjoyed our new home. Another social life started in Haslemere and we made a lot of friends, knowing it wouldn't last forever. The following year, when Mark started school, I soon got to know the mothers of Mark's pals at Bramshott Chase School, which instantly opened up a whole new social circle. A few doors away, we discovered an old theatre friend of Jim's, a writer named Richard Ward, who was part of the touring company Century Theatre. Opposite us was Jesse Mann's timber mill and in the thatched cottage next to it was Mrs Wadey, a delightful lady who became a great help and friend. Her family owned and ran the timber mill and she knew everyone. We did quite a lot of entertaining – I was always having people round, particularly Jim's friends and colleagues – and sometimes we'd go up to London to see our showbiz friends at the weekend.

I was never bored because there was always too much to do, even with the help of Mrs Hammond, a lovely lady from another part of the village who came in every day. She and her family helped us out with babysitting and so many other things – I was very grateful to have found them. But when we were first married, we didn't have much money, and in that situation you've got to do things for yourself. I don't know how mothers manage to work these days, because gardening, housework, carpentry, looking after children, cooking, dressmaking and everything else is a full-time job, although people don't seem to think it is any more. The times are different.

Our daughter Claire was born in February 1959 and when Rose followed twenty-one months later our family was complete. But now that there were five of us, we needed more than a bicycle to get around. Although we were on a good bus route, I was keen to get a car, so when a distant uncle left me some money, there was only one thing I wanted to spend it on!

I bought a 1946 Rover 16 from Mann's Garage in Chiddingfold for £255, on the advice of a neighbour who was a schoolmaster. I had never owned a car, so he kindly sat with me as I drove all round the local roads and got to know how the car handled the bumps and hairpin bends. I felt like a beginner and was tempted to put on 'L' plates, because it was so long since I had passed my test in Reading, but I soon got the hang of it and have never forgotten all the tips he gave me for safe but fast driving.

Perhaps I became a little too confident, because one day I came home and drove rather flamboyantly into our wooden garage, knocking the back wall. Now, it happened that the previous owner of the house had been a naval man and had erected a flagpole just behind the garage. It was quite old and must have been a bit rotten, because it came down with a resounding crack across the lawn. Timber! Luckily, there was no damage done, apart from to the flagpole, which subsequently made good firewood.

Now it was Jim's turn to learn to drive. Although he had flown planes in the war and gained his pilot's licence at the age of sixteen, he hadn't got his driving licence. To his relief, he passed first time – in hilly, traffic-congested Guildford. But when he got in the car to come home, it refused to start. Typical. This was the first of many 'adventures' we had with second-hand cars.

Eventually he got it started and came happily home on his own, very pleased with himself. At last we were properly mobile and could travel the country exploring and visiting friends. Having a car was going to make an enormous difference to our lives. We were full of hope and optimism.

EIGHT

Green and White Striped Dress

Jim's secretary came into work from her home in Buckinghamshire one day with the news that the local hunt had killed a vixen and left three cubs, which would probably be kept to grow up and then hunted. 'Will you take one and rescue it?' she asked Jim.

This was how we acquired Vicky, who arrived home with Jim in an old tin hatbox. He set about making a run for her on our outside covered terrace, just beyond the sitting-room French doors and windows – and when she settled down and became a bit tame, we would bring her indoors for a change.

Vicky was tremendous fun for the short time we had her, but you had to watch her. I wasn't terribly pleased to find her chewing a dress of green and white striped cotton that I was making for my daughter Claire, after I'd put it down for a moment. It was just an ordinary girl's dress with a bodice and slightly gathered skirt, but even so! However, you couldn't be cross with Vicky for long. She was so sweet and impish. She often played with Honey, our golden Labrador puppy, another new acquisition, and I loved to watch them frolicking. We used to take them both for walks on a lead.

One afternoon, Vicky was indoors when a rather 'proper' lady neighbour called in. We were instantly on our best behaviour because she was very stiff and starchy. Just as I was offering her a cup of tea, Vicky popped her head out from under the sofa to see who had arrived. Our neighbour must have seen her, but she pretended she hadn't and completely ignored her. In the long moments that followed, nobody said anything. Jim and I were trying hard to keep a straight face – and who knows what our neighbour was thinking. A fox cub in the house? Perhaps she thought she was seeing things and couldn't believe her eyes. Although not unheard of, it certainly was not the norm to have a pet fox in the house!

We would have loved to keep Vicky, but when she was six months old we thought it was probably time for her to go back to the wild. It was January and mating time for foxes, so we left her cage open and waited to see what she would do. At first she kept coming back, but her visits became fewer and at last she disappeared altogether. We dearly hoped that she had survived and found a mate in the woods beyond our garden.

About a year or so later, Jim and his mother, Myra, were taking Honey for a walk in the woods one evening when Honey surprised a fox – but the fox did not run away. It stopped in the middle of a clearing to let Honey come up and touch noses! And then it was gone. Was it Vicky? We always liked to think so.

Honey was with us for fourteen years and became a beloved family friend. When we first had her, just six weeks old and the 'runt' of the litter, costing 3 guineas, she could barely climb the rather steep edge onto the lawn. But she rapidly grew and with the help of our gardener, Bloxham, an ex-gamekeeper, became an excellent gun dog. We found her a pedigree mate and she had two litters of eight adorable puppies, which was heaven, especially for the children. We easily found homes for them, selling them for 10 and 12 guineas a time and putting the proceeds towards our very first washing machine. Words cannot express quite how wonderful it was to relinquish three young children's washing to a 'state-of-the-art' twin-tub Hoovermatic. I used it constantly as they grew up, until it was finally replaced by a modern front loader in the late 1980s.

At the time, Jim was very keen on making ginger beer – a popular hobby then – and he stored the bottles on the shelf above the washing machine. One afternoon, I heard the most almighty explosion from the next room. Goodness, I thought, the washing machine has blown up. But no, it was the bottles of ginger beer, which had blown their corks and, in doing so, knocked all the saucepans off the shelf above. It took absolutely ages to clear up the mess, but we did laugh!

As well as his other programmes, Jim worked on a few promotional shows that were known as 'Ad Mags' and very often he would return home with some of the leftover products – usually food. One night he came back with a briefcase full of different sorts of sausages, some very garlicky and smelly, but nevertheless welcome. He was offered plenty of other things, too, but Jim never wanted his ethics called into question so he usually turned them down, often to the disappointment of the rest of the family!

At work Jim was always very principled. At home, however, he was a little more relaxed. When he got permission to do some rough shooting, Bloxham taught him what to do and helped him buy a gun. Rough shooting licences were generally issued to help farmers keep the pigeon population down and once Jim had his, he would regularly come home with a pigeon or two for supper. One early morning, he shot a pheasant by mistake – accidentally on purpose – and put it in his carrier bag, but the bird's handsome tail feathers didn't fit and weren't tucked in properly. On his way home, he passed the local bobby and, although he knew him well, Jim couldn't help feeling a little warm under the collar. The rough shooting licence definitely didn't extend to pheasants.

He needn't have worried. 'Pigeons have got very long feathers this season, haven't they?' the police constable remarked drily, before going on his way!

After being in London, we really appreciated country life. Our garden sloped down to the River Wey, which was beautiful, although we had to put up a fence to stop the children going too near its banks and falling in, especially since Claire was delightedly learning to walk and Rose was in the pushchair. There were trout in the river and we still tease Mark about the day he caught his first fish. He was very pleased with himself, but couldn't bring himself to eat it for supper! We had friends with a pony across the road and Mark learned to ride a little. And a family up the lane had a smallholding with ponies, pigs, chickens and boxer dogs – quite a menagerie – and we had a lot of fun with them too.

One of the perks of Jim doing outside broadcasts with ATV was that sometimes we would all go along for the outing. Polo at Windsor was a favourite, as we could all run about among the rhododendrons in Savill Gardens while Jim was busy. We would watch Prince Philip playing polo and try to spot the Queen in the distance – and the children played endless games of roly-poly down the sloping lawns in their 'best' clothes. These weren't anything particularly special, just a little bit nicer than usual, and clean – to start with, anyway!

I always made sure Mark and the girls were well turned out when it mattered. I couldn't have faced Mummy if they weren't, as she inspected them closely when she came to visit – and we saw a lot more of her after my father died in 1960. Although we had seen them fairly frequently before that, Mummy was busy caring for my father, who became quite ill in his final years, and I was preoccupied with looking after a husband and small children.

I knitted clothes for the children and made little outfits – and we were given new clothes and lots of hand-me-downs. When Mark wasn't in his school uniform, he wore knee-length shorts and shirts. Someone gave him a very smart sailor suit, but I'm not sure he was all that keen on it. Of course, my mother and I loved him in it. The girls had knee-length skirts, button-up blouses and cardigans, and for parties and special occasions I made them a couple of frilly dresses that weren't a million miles from the ones I wore as a child.

There was a long succession of Clarks shoes in different sizes. Clarks are one of the only brands I remember being aware of then, because branded clothing lines for children weren't a big thing. It's easy to forget that Gap only introduced their children's line in 1986, followed by Baby Gap in 1990. Before that, children didn't have their own mainstream fashions and styles – at least not to the extent they do now.

Nobody I knew dressed their children in designer clothes. Maybe the very rich did, but no normal person had that sort of money. I certainly didn't. I was far too busy focusing on bringing them up, which involved a lot of scrimping and saving and making something out of nothing. These days I don't much like seeing pictures of 'celebrity children' dressed in designer labels. It seems ridiculous to spend that kind of money on something that's only going to last a few months.

I was thinking about this just recently when I came across a children's fashion shoot in one of those free glossy magazines that gets delivered through your door. It featured rather ordinary-looking toddlers' party dresses for £750 apiece – and it wasn't even a fashion magazine. I thought it must be a misprint, but there were several outfits in a similar price range, which I found extraordinary.

By 1962, after four years in Haslemere, we couldn't put off moving any longer. We had to find somewhere more convenient for the ATV studios in Borehamwood now that Jim had been put in charge of his department and promoted to Head Floor Manager. It was a horrible journey from Haslemere to Hertfordshire and one or two others doing similar daily drives had either been killed in a crash or overwhelmed by stress and exhaustion. There was no alternative but to move, which was a shame as we had settled very happily and loved our home and life in Surrey.

And so began the interesting but rather arduous process of house hunting in another county. We looked at hundreds of houses, which was not altogether easy with three young children to look after. The upside was that we learned a lot about Hertfordshire, but as time began to run out, we hastily settled on a spacious period house in the village of Kimpton, near the old A1 and within reasonable distance of the studios and several ATV friends who lived in the area.

Our house in Haslemere took a long time to sell and we had to take out a painful bridging loan to move into the Old White House in Kimpton High Street in the July. Our new home was a rambling old place with a Tudor front, a Victorian back and a large double garage that opened onto the pretty village green and the quiet lane leading up to the church. A huge recreation ground immediately opposite the house compensated for its tiny garden – there was a playground and lots of space for dogs and children.

Kimpton was a much more peaceful place in the 1960s than it is today. Now it's near the A1M and Luton airport, so there's a lot more hustle and bustle. Everyone was very welcoming and it wasn't long before we made some life-long friends and found people to help in the house and with the children. We found a pre-prep school for Mark in Harpenden and the girls went to the nursery school in the British Legion Hall across the road. They all settled really quickly and loved all the usual childhood things such as painting and drawing. Playing on the swings at the top of the playground was also a hugely popular pastime for the children, along with making mud pies under the hedge. Later the girls went to the village school just a few minutes' walk along the High Street. We shared Mark's school run with other parents, so on the whole we were quite organized.

Silvie was the first of a series of au pairs who came to live with us. A French girl from a well-off family in Nantes, she stayed for about a year while she went to college in St Albans to study English. However, she already spoke English quite fluently on arrival and was willing and helpful, so she was a real asset to have around. When it came to her time to leave, her father wanted her to have her own car, so Jim duly took her to a showroom in Berkeley Square to buy an MGB sports car. It was far beyond anything we could afford, which is rather funny when you think about it.

Silvie was our first and favourite au pair and we kept in touch for many years. We were lucky to find another 'treasure' in the form of Mrs Warner, who lived near us in the village and was always on hand to help with everything. Mrs Warner had a sunny disposition to match her rosy complexion. A down-to-earth country person, with no aspirations over the horizon or beyond the village boundaries, she was much more than a daily help with the domestic chores. She was wonderful with the children, who were always happy to be with her.

*

The winter of 1963 was the coldest winter of the century, and England was covered in a thick blanket of snow. Since Kimpton is in a hollow, the whole place was completely snowed in. It was just impossible to get past the hills at either end of the village. It was so bad that Jim could not get to the Palladium – the only time he didn't make it in twelve years. There were lots of shops in the village in those days, so we didn't starve. Our little enclave took on a holiday atmosphere and people really let their hair down. The recreation ground was on a nice slope and there was lots of tobogganing – I even pulled the children to school on our sledge.

Jim had a lot of work on at the time. As well as *Sunday Night at the London Palladium*, he was doing a range of light entertainment shows appropriate to his background in variety, dance and comedy. These were filmed at the old Wood Green Empire and sometimes I used to go along to watch, often taking a friend.

One evening I was having a cup of tea in the canteen with one such friend when she turned to me and said, 'Do they really allow tramps in here?'

'What do you mean?' I asked.

She motioned to a very dishevelled chap sitting near us, unaware that it was the well-known actor Dermot Kelly, dressed for his part playing a tramp on *The Arthur Haynes Show* and staying in character while he had a bite to eat!

A couple of weeks later, just after Jim had gone to work, one of his colleagues phoned up and asked me to be an extra on this very same *Arthur Haynes Show*. I thought it might be fun, so I left my au pair to hold the fort at home and went along to the Wood Green Empire. Jim was the floor manager that day and he was understandably surprised to see me.

'What are you doing here?' he asked.

'I'm working!' I announced.

And so began my career as an extra – once I'd spoken to the other extras and found out how to get myself an agent, that is. It was the perfect job to slot into family life, as it was just the odd day or two, here and there – and as the children grew older, I began to do a bit more. I branched out into commercials, a little modelling and, later, films. I enjoyed it enormously and Jim liked me doing it too, as he could see how happy it made me.

Around the same time, I applied to the top model agencies, as I thought it might be fun to be back in that world, too. But nobody liked the look of me. It was the era of Jean Shrimpton – soon to be joined by Twiggy – which was not my 'look' at all. My face did not fit! Perhaps my figure wasn't boyish enough; my age may also have been a factor. The new models personified what Diana Vreeland, *Vogue*'s editor-in-chief, dubbed the 'youthquake'. Young people had spending power, and youth culture was beginning to dominate like never before. Suddenly a huge division sprang up between 'young' and 'old' fashions.

Although Jean Shrimpton was doing *Vogue* covers in the early 1960s, the real turning point came when André Courrèges unveiled his spring 1964 collection, which had a similar kind of seismic effect on the fashion world as Dior's New Look in 1947. Courrèges's short, geometrically shaped shift dresses were a sensation. A year later, Yves Saint Laurent produced his iconic 'Mondrian' day dresses, using thick black lines and colour blocks printed on densely woven wool jersey. I thought they were fabulous.

Since I can wear anything and always have been able to, I wasn't afraid of the new silhouette. In fact, I was quite happy to wear something that skimmed my hips. The new shift dress had a waist, but it wasn't delineated as it had been in the 1950s and some were straighter than others, so I always used to put darts in mine to make them look a bit shaped. Then I'd put a border on the hem, a frill or some lace – whatever suited.

My dressmaking skills were steadily improving with practice. I didn't have any lessons, but I often picked up tips from magazines – and from friends, of course. A lot of people sewed in those days, so we were always talking about the clothes we were making and showing each other little tricks and shortcuts. You could buy patterns and material in village shops as well as department stores

– pattern-book browsing was another form of window shopping then.

Crimplene was a popular material for making shift dresses because its dense weave and wrinkle-resistant surface helped to maintain the structure of the dress as you wore it, just like the (more expensive) thick cottons and wools used by Courrèges and Saint Laurent. Crimplene fell out of fashion in the 1970s when lighter-weave polyester fabrics became popular, but it's actually fantastic for dressmaking and never loses its shape. I still wear a pair of black crimplene trousers that I bought in the 1970s. In fact, I wore them along to a big H&M campaign shoot in Stockholm recently, because they're the most comfortable trousers in my wardrobe and still smart after all these years.

I made a lovely white crimplene shift dress to wear to a show at the Palladium. It had a trim of feathers on the bottom that I'd bought as a strip and sewn on. Just as I was about to set off, Claire, who had been playing in the garden, came up and said, 'Goodbye, Mummy!' and put a perfect muddy handprint right in the middle of it. Oh dear! But, because it was crimplene, I was able to wash off the mud and go on my way with a wet dress. By the time I got to London, it was dry. Whatever you think of crimplene, you can't knock its 'wash and wear' properties.

My embossed cotton 'going away' outfit from my

wedding was suddenly back in fashion, so I wore it to a cocktail party at the Savoy. But instead of the black sandals I'd worn in 1954, this time I teamed it with white ankle boots. My inspiration was a photograph I'd seen of a model wearing ankle boots with a Courrèges dress – I decided it was a really good look and headed straight to Freeman, Hardy and Willis to get a pair in white. They looked terribly dashing with my white jacket and skirt! What's more, they had a flat heel and were very comfortable. This was a huge bonus, because I've never been into high heels.

Although the new trends influenced me, I wasn't a slavish follower of fashion. I've always just picked out what suits me. That's the trick – it's about finding what looks good on you. So although I used to go into Mary Quant's shop to have a browse, I don't remember buying anything, except perhaps a lipstick or two. Someone gave me a Mary Quant dress once but it didn't suit me and I never liked it. It was orange and black with frills down the front and on the edge of the sleeves – the height of fashion – but it was a bit too 'Laura Ashley' for me, so I got rid of it.

I wore miniskirts, but not super-short ones. I was aware that I wasn't in my twenties and so was a little circumspect, although I never gave much thought to my age. In those days, nobody actually mentioned their age. You didn't talk about it. I never knew how old Mummy was until she got really old. Then she was proud of it, as I am now.

I stuck with the agents who put me up for jobs as an extra throughout the 1960s and did a few advertising modelling jobs. Although I'd thought it might be fun to do some more modelling, it was no big deal when the modelling agencies turned me down; and even if age had been a factor along with my 'unfashionable' looks, it certainly didn't make me worry – it was just one of those things! Posing with other models beside various beds for a Dunlopillo catalogue was a nice day's work and I did a couple of shoots for *Woman's Journal*. For another job, I colluded in a rather dubious trick of the trade that always made me laugh – the perennial Alston's Corsets adverts. This was a black-and-white photograph of women portrayed 'before' and 'after' wearing corsets. Being slim, I was the 'after' picture. They called me 'Mrs B. C. from Biggleswade' – and now that I actually live not far from Biggleswade this seems doubly amusing.

One job that particularly sticks in my mind is an advertisement for Kellogg's Corn Flakes. Knowing I could ride, my agent put me up for it – I was commissioned to gallop across Wimbledon Common with a young girl on a horse beside me, before posing with her for a breakfast scene eating the cornflakes. Well, although the girl had said she could ride, it turned out that she quite obviously could not and I had a very hairy morning trying to ride two horses at once. In the end I told her just to hold the saddle and I would guide the horse along. Fortunately, it looked fine in the photograph.

When we arrived to do the interior scene at the studio, the photographer turned out to be the husband of an old school friend, so it was quite a day. I just love how you never know who you are going to meet on a modelling job: new friends, old friends and numerous friends of friends! Claire and Rose happily joined me in some of the photographs and background commercials. They always enjoyed it, but I didn't want them to do too much modelling as Jim and I felt it was important for them to have as normal a childhood as possible. Even Honey got in on the act once, when she was photographed for a camera leaflet licking an ice cream – Labrador heaven!

I had to wear my own clothes for nearly all my photographic and television jobs, so a large assortment was essential. It went on your CV: 'Good wardrobe – evening, furs, sports clothes, etc.' Most of the time you were asked to wear 'smart casual' and I am still not sure exactly what that is. It can be interpreted in so many ways and seems to cover a multitude of sins. For television, you needed 'quiet' clothes and so I made several suits, including a tweed suit in cream and white check. Flamboyance was the last thing the producers wanted in their extras, so my 'Shocking Pink' lipstick remained in my handbag until the end of the day.

Eventually, I had acquired several different agents for television, film extra work and modelling. Most of the time it worked out and the jobs didn't clash, but sometimes dates or locations changed at the last minute, which meant juggling furiously and trying not to upset any of the agents. Being of a reliable and conscientious nature, and wanting to be as professional as I could, I always found it a bit stressful trying to manage things that were beyond my control. Still, we all had a similar problem and just had to get on with it – and things always seemed to work out in the end.

Life became even busier when Jim and a few other members of the village decided to revive the traditional May Day Festival, which had not been celebrated in Kimpton for many years. They drew on the knowledge and memories of people whose families had been in the village a long time and, after many meetings and allocations of duties, all that was left to do was to find a celebrity to open the fair – adding a modern flourish to an ancient tradition.

Jim obviously knew a few well-known people, but he really pulled out a trump card when he persuaded the comedian Eric Morecambe to kick off the proceedings in 1966. Jim had worked with Eric, who lived locally, and his daughter went to the same school as our son, Mark, so he was the ideal candidate. Eric and his television partner,

Ernie Wise, were a hugely popular comedy double act at the time – and would remain so. I still love them and their humour. Their madcap sketches featuring celebrities were so funny and somehow innocent. It all went off splendidly. There was a carnival procession through the village, with floats representing the local clubs, pubs and businesses. There were stalls with games, produce and books, fancy-dress competitions and pony rides. There were teas in various houses in the village and a 'barrel race', a tug of war and, of course, a traditional Punch and Judy show put on by the famous Professor Des Turner, aided by his wife Mavis. After Eric Morecambe had crowned the May Queen – a proud fifteen-year-old, resplendent in her white dress – she and her attendants paraded in a line of vintage cars provided by Vauxhall (who had a large manufacturing base in nearby Luton).

Everyone in the village contributed to making the first festival a success and more events were added in subsequent years, including art exhibitions in the church and a display from local archives on show in the church hall. These days it has extended to take in the whole Bank Holiday weekend. It became a highlight of the year, but a very busy time, what with making fancy-dress costumes, baking for the teas and produce stalls and entertaining the celebrities, not to mention setting up the stalls and making the floats! Sometimes the weather was kind, but May can be unpredictable and it was not uncommon to see poor little 'fairies' shivering on the floats, looking very miserable and damp in their flimsy gauze and chiffon outfits.

We had not been in Kimpton very long when we realized that we had bitten off more than we could chew with regards to our house. It seemed sensible to cut our losses and move to somewhere more viable and affordable to give us the time we needed to find our 'ideal' home in Hertfordshire. We settled on a potentially more desirable modern house in Hollybush Close in Old Welwyn. We moved there in the summer of 1967, thinking we would only be there for a short while, but it turned out to be so convenient for the children's schools and Jim's work that we ended up staying for nine years.

It was very cramped after the Old White House and the girls had to share until we converted an eaves storeroom into a tiny single room for Claire, which she loved as long as she didn't sit up too quickly in bed and bump her head on the ceiling. The garage was like so many then – there was just enough room to drive the car into it, but not to open the door to get out of it! (Instead we used it as a storeroom and sloe gin- and wine-making area.) But the garden was a decent size and we all appreciated having somewhere the children could play, I could garden and Jim could tend a vegetable patch. Mark had Omo, a white mouse, who caused much merriment running along the landing in his wheel. Claire and Rose had various guinea pigs, including Patch and Alberta, and a rabbit named

Snowy. We found a cute kitten from the local saw mill and named her Cinders, but sadly she did not last long, as she used to follow the girls to school at the bottom of the road and one morning failed to make it back through the traffic.

One of the girls found a baby rook who'd fallen out of his nest and named him 'Johnny the Rook'. Johnny used to perch on the rose pergola on the patio and we fed him on dog food. He didn't come indoors, but was really friendly and used to jump on my back at every opportunity. The only problem with this was that his claws were excruciatingly painful if I was in a bikini! (As I loved to be when it was hot enough.) He was very cheeky – as fast as I tidied the fallen rose petals into my garden trug, he would throw them out again! Still, he was always good company, even when he was up to his tricks, and we looked after him until he was able to fly away.

I hardly worked over the next few years, as I wanted to be with the children, especially over the move. Claire and Rose, however, got around far more than I did, going on school trips to Guernsey and Wales, among other places. Jim's twelve-year stint at *Sunday Night at the London Palladium* came to an end when ATV lost its London weekend franchise and the shake-up of the commercial television companies that followed led to industrial unrest. I began to wonder, even worry, about what the future held and how we would manage financially. I wasn't quite sure how much work either of us could count on in the years to come. So I started to think about what else I could do to earn a living.

As I was picking the girls up from school one afternoon, one of the other mothers looked at me and said, 'I love your dress. Did you get it in Welwyn?'

'I made it,' I said, feeling quite pleased with myself.

'Ooh, would you be able to make one for me?' she asked. 'I'm hopeless at things like that. I'd be so grateful – and I'd pay you the going rate.'

Why not? I thought. I enjoyed dressmaking and could do it at home, so it was the perfect way for me to bolster the family finances.

'I'd love to!' I told her, and within no time I was earning money making clothes, along with a whole set of new acquaintances. I was glad of the extra income and, being the social animal that I am, even gladder about my growing network of clients, who soon became firm friends!

NINE

Home-made Hot Pants

Mary Quant started the craze for hot pants in the late 1960s – she was very good at launching trends. They were considered quite daring at the time, but weren't anywhere near as revealing as the frayed denim cut-offs people wear today, which I'm not terribly fond of. Hot pants then were more like beach shorts – they had a jaunty innocence about them – and along with everybody else, I happily wore them, usually with a long cardigan or coat. I made several pairs for friends. Like trousers, they weren't too difficult to make when you knew how, although they could be a bit fiddly. Bikinis were much trickier. I made two or three bikinis, but only for myself. Bought swimwear was better.

We were lucky that we could spend our summer family holidays either with my mother, who had now moved to Worthing in Sussex, or with Jim's mother and stepfather, Myra and Richard, in West Looe in Cornwall. Myra and Richard's cottage was tiny, so it was a bit of a squash and we generally tried to make sure that we were not all there all the time. Jim couldn't join us for the entire school holidays so sometimes we'd go when he was working, or when one or two of the children were off on expeditions or school trips. Later on, we rented a separate house, which made things easier.

Myra had a little motorboat called *Lollipop* and either she or Richard would take us out in it. We were always happier when it was Myra at the helm, because Richard was an unpredictable navigator and we were never sure if we would get back to port! Looe was, and still is, a centre for shark fishing, and one of the highlights of each day was to watch the fishing boats come into the harbour. We'd look out for the number of yellow flags attached to the masts, which denoted how many sharks had been caught, and then go down to see how big they were – the children especially loved to see the day's catch. There were lots of other fish besides, of course, as Looe was a busy port. Myra knew some of the fishermen well, so we often had fresh mackerel for tea.

A favourite pastime for Jim and Claire was looking for butterflies up in the fields behind Myra and Richard's cottage. We went on long walks – some sunny, some rainy and windswept – and explored other villages and land-marks along the coast. Passing Poldhu one day, the site of some of Marconi's groundbreaking experiments with shortwave radio, I was amused to think that this eminent man with his name on several road signs had once greatly admired my mother. Of course, the children were far more interested in the Monkey Sanctuary near Looe, which was an intriguing place – there were monkeys literally all over the place and all over you!

One April, we borrowed a neighbour's bungalow at Bacton on the Norfolk coast. It was a very cold bungalow with thin walls, so we went out as much as possible! We discovered the Broads at Hickling and Horsey Mere, with their spectacular windmills, and the wonderful long beach at Holkham, strewn with shells. My parents had spent some of their honeymoon at Mundesley and had walked to the village of Trunch, so we did that too. Jim had been researching our family trees and, knowing that my father's ancestors came from East Anglia, we spent an afternoon looking for graves at Hindolveston and North Elmham. Eventually we found some in North Elmham that were in the process of being bulldozed, so we were only just in time. They were later rearranged around the walls of the churchyard, though I am not sure how many remained intact.

Best of all was the Thursford Museum, which housed a collection of old fairground organs, roundabouts and paraphernalia owned by George Cushing. In those days it was just a huge barn full of stuff he had collected – and he happily showed us round, telling us all about it and working the various organs and mechanical toys. Now it is a big business and has an enormous show every Christmas.

We had a very different kind of holiday when we went

to stay with my mother in Worthing. Although we were still 'beside the seaside', it couldn't have been more different from the wild Cornish coastline or the flat Norfolk seascape. The beach at Worthing was wonderful and we also explored inland; one of the nicest walks we used to do with the children was through the big cemetery near Findon. Cemeteries tend to be beautiful, unspoilt, interesting places, full of wildlife and flowers – and, apart from the really famous ones like Highgate in London and Père Lachaise in Paris, they're rarely overcrowded.

I will never forget visiting Potter's Museum at Bramber, which contained the extraordinary life's work of Walter Potter, a nineteenth-century English taxidermist. Some people may have found it gruesome, but it was a fascinating relic of a bygone age. Potter made intricate tableaux peopled with small stuffed animals. They were very whimsical and depicted scenes from English life: a guinea pigs' cricket match; a schoolroom full of forty-six stuffed baby rabbits at their desks; a rats' gambling den; a squirrels' drinking party; and the tale of Cock Robin re-enacted in a glass case.

Perhaps the most elaborate was the kittens' wedding, which featured twenty stuffed kittens wearing traditional late-nineteenth-century morning suits and brocade dresses, with the bride in a lace veil carrying a posy of orange blossoms. Potter's daughter and one of his neighbours made the costumes and they're very cleverly done. The museum closed in the 1970s and I lost sight of the collection, which resurfaced in 2003 when it was auctioned off by Bonhams and dispersed. For some reason, Damien Hirst's offer to buy the whole lot for a million pounds, just to keep the collection together, was rejected. It seemed a shame to divide it up.

As the girls grew older, we would have trips to Brighton and wander around the small shops and boutiques in the Lanes. One of our rituals was to go to a favourite Italian cafe, where we would buy ice creams and sorbet such as we had never seen before, in real, hollowed-out oranges and other exotic shapes! Claire and Rose thought it such a treat and very Mediterranean. Then we would go on the hunt for clothes. The girls were now in their early teens, and had inherited many of my and Jim's features – they shared Jim's colouring with their blonde wavy hair and they had my blue eyes. They were often mistaken for twins – and still are! However, Claire's physique is more like mine, tall and slim with broad shoulders, while Rose is more curvy, like my mother Irene was. Now interested in their wardrobes, we had a lot of fun looking for the latest trends and bargains. They always had a strong sense of their own style – and still do. The only time I withheld my approval was when Rose was about fourteen and went through what she now calls her 'Bowie years'; she cut her hair short and dyed it orange, which I didn't like at all!

Fashion was a mix of many styles in the 1970s, which

meant there was much greater freedom of choice. The differing fashion identities coming out of London, Paris and New York early on in the decade encouraged an eclectic approach, and you felt you could draw on anything from the 'hippy' look to the 1920s revival. In sharp contrast to the geometric lines and shapes of a few years previously, the silhouette was becoming longer and more fluid. There was less flesh on show, and more of what I would call romance. Fabric started appearing in softer tones and colours, replacing the psychedelics and pastels of the late 1960s. Paisley, for example, had come back rather glaringly in 1967 and was pretty awful. Now it settled into richer, more muted tones.

This was also the era of flared trousers and bell-bottoms, of which I had several pairs. These could be quite dangerous, as they were very long and flared out at the knee, and could easily trip you up in a high wind. Good luck to the people wearing loon pants, which had an even wider circumference at the bottom! I haven't kept any boots from the 1970s, but I remember preferring the low-heeled styles that came up to just below the knee – I didn't go in for lace-up 'granny boots'. Most of all I liked Hush Puppies. They were such comfortable shoes.

The hippy look, when it was done well, reminded me of Edith Sitwell's style in the 1950s, which I had so admired. Embroidered shirts and what were known as 'Mexican peasant blouses' were all the rage, as were floppy hats and boaters. I wore (and still wear) a lot of midi- and maxi-length skirts and dresses, sometimes coordinating them with a chunky knit, my favourite being a purple midi-length cardigan that I still wear today. Knitwear was another huge trend of the decade and there were a lot of statement jumpers out there, some of them gorgeous and others quite ghastly. So many fashion experiments went wrong in those days, but elements of what we wore in the Seventies are constantly being revived. A few years ago I wore a wonderful hippyish dress for a Wunderkind campaign and I'm a big fan of Etro – both these labels show the influence of that decade.

About two years ago I bought a fabulous 1970s Monsoon dress at a Macmillan coffee morning and another at a vintage sale. They're both very colourful and 'out there' – not the kind of thing I'd wear in my local high street, but I've worn them to several special occasions. It's a wonderful feeling to discover a gem when you least expect it and to support a worthwhile charity in the process. Monsoon was great in the 1970s and I also loved Biba, but I didn't shop there as I didn't have a lot of money to throw around while I was bringing up the children. Although I look back on the era's fashion with fondness and tried to keep up with the latest trends, family life always came first.

My car then was a Ford 'Pop', or Popular, one of the best and most reliable cars I'd had. It was so simple, like a sewing machine! The only problem was that it was a bit high off the ground and rather unstable in the wind. I had one particularly alarming drive along the coast road from Brighton to Hastings in a gale, constantly worried about being blown from one side of the road to the other, and back again. I crept along, concentrating hard, from one central road marking to the next.

We had some awful second-hand cars before that, chief of which was a pale blue Standard. It was just a rust box on wheels, so cold and uncomfortable on a long journey. Driving to Cornwall was grim – it took twice as long as it does now, you could feel every bump in the road and the children were all travel sick. To while away the time, we'd play car games like I Spy and the pub sign game, where you would take turns to watch excitedly for the next pub sign to pass and add up how many legs its name contained. So, the White Lion had four and the Coach and Horses had sixteen (that usually made you a winner).

We were heartily glad when we said goodbye to the Standard. Cars were so much more unreliable in those days and they always seemed to be breaking down. Since the children perpetually needed fetching or rescuing, engine trouble made life even more hectic. Jim eventually went on to Volvos and I had a series of Ford Cortinas, which were a big improvement.

*

I was still dressmaking and my skills were steadily improving as I made more clothes for friends and acquaintances. One friend Kathleen had several lengths of Bernard Klein tweed, which was absolutely lovely to look at, but very hairy and terrible to sew. Still, it was good experience. I made lots of tweed skirts for her and she's still got them – unfortunately she can't get into them any more, but she can't bear to part with them.

Shift dresses and flared skirts were always in demand, and I often made outfits for special occasions, including several evening gowns and a flamenco-style wedding dress for a friend, which had endless fiddly frills on the skirt. It was less expensive then to buy material and make your own unique clothes. The price of fabric has soared in the decades since and we live in the age of Primark, TK Maxx and multiple charity shops on every high street, so there's less incentive to get out your sewing machine. Yet, despite it all, there has been a sewing renaissance in recent years, perhaps because the machines are so clever these days and you can even learn to sew online!

On top of the dressmaking in 1971, other work came along, too – my agents knew that I had modelled in the 1950s and now I was asked to do 'store modelling'. This meant walking around the restaurants of many big department stores at coffee, lunch and teatime, wearing a particular brand of clothes, carrying a card with the designer's name on it to advertise my presence, and talking to the customers. It was a lot of fun and really did sell the clothes – women of all shapes and sizes often bought a suit or coat because they thought it looked good on me. It also fitted in with the children's school hours, more or less, as it was ten to four, three days a week. Even factoring in the travelling time, it was quite manageable, especially as the children were getting older. It was even more convenient when I was at the Welwyn Department Stores – now John Lewis – which was just down the road.

I was 'Miss Dannimac' regularly from 1972 to 1984 and, fairly soon after I started, the Berkertex area manageress saw me and asked me to work for her as well. Norman Hartnell was no longer at Berkertex, but the clothes remained classic and stylish and I enjoyed wearing them. I don't know why I was chosen for the job. I suppose that some people can make clothes look better than others. Having broad shoulders helps, I think, but posture also makes a big difference. If you hunch, nothing looks any good. If you stand upright, it makes a fantastic difference and whatever you're wearing looks so much better!

I also worked for Alexon women's fashions and Astraka's fake-fur coats and jackets – Astraka were one of the first fashion labels to use faux fur – and modelled hats and jewellery as well as clothes. I usually did six weeks in the spring and autumn and a few days in the run-up to

Christmas or at sale times. Sometimes I did promotions for other products, like wines, bacon and cheese, although this didn't require walking around the restaurants but standing in one location encouraging people to look and try!

I found myself travelling all over the south-east – to London, Brent Cross, Enfield, Watford, High Wycombe, Romford, Luton, Bedford, Cambridge and more. Sometimes the winter weather made journeys hazardous and I remember a particularly dicey journey to Luton in the snow one April. The most enjoyable part of the job was making new friends – and I often stayed with old friends when I had to travel long distances, so it was always a sociable time.

As 'Miss Berkertex' in the 1950s, I went to Broadstairs, Bournemouth, Harrogate and Busby's of Bradford to do fashion shows. I had a wonderful time in Bradford, where I stayed at the Midland Hotel. When I wasn't working, the Busbys showed me the countryside around Bradford and I fell in love with the moors that had so inspired the Brontë sisters. To me, each feature of the landscape looked as if it had been outlined with a black crayon, and I was desperate to get sketching as soon as I got back to the hotel. In the evenings, the Busbys took me to the theatre, to dances, and into their home – they were incredibly hospitable in the northern English tradition, and really made me feel like one of the family.

Another time in the 1950s I went to Matthias Robinson in Leeds to show the latest Berkertex range. I stayed at the Hotel Metropole, where I had my first Turkish bath – not something I had expected in Leeds! I also did some shows in Hull, where the people I worked for gave me a wonderful time. One evening I was taken to a tiny pub on Spurn Head, the southernmost tip of a narrow sand peninsula on the East Riding coast. It was a very bleak place and the pub was full of such fascinating characters that I made some sketches of them, which I still have.

I was glad of the little I was able to contribute to the family finances through my store modelling and extra work, especially after Jim suffered a mild heart attack in 1974. It was a wake-up call and although he recovered well, he initially went back to work on a part-time basis, as no one wanted him to take any risks with his health. We wanted to get him back to normal and full fitness but he loved his work too much to stop.

Things became difficult in other ways at ATV during that time, with wrangles between union and management and several 'wildcat' strikes, culminating in a big union walkout at the studios in 1974. Filming came to a halt and Jim and many of his colleagues had nothing to do but wait, hoping for a resolution. When they eventually went back, the terms of employment had changed and his work became more sporadic. These were worrying times for us.

I worked as often as I could, but had enough free time to do O-level Cookery at the local college in Welwyn Garden City. My mother had taught me how to cook, so I had always managed, but I thought it would be good to improve my skills. It was quite an effort, what with having to provide all the ingredients, prepare the recipes to a rigid timetable and carry the results home – very different from our cookery lessons at school with Scottish Miss Blair all those years before! We students got very hot and bothered, but it was quite fun having something new to feed to the family each week and I actually managed to pass the exam too. I made all my own aprons and some for friends. Unlike bikinis, home-made aprons tend to be a lot better than bought ones.

While Jim was recovering, my mother had yet another in a series of falls and decided that she'd had enough of living on her own. Over the years, she had fallen over the mower, the cat and umpteen other things, breaking her wrist several times. Now in her early eighties, she had what was then called 'brittle bones' and is now better known as osteoporosis. In the circumstances, it seemed a good idea to sell our respective houses and buy a bigger one for all of us, so we began the fascinating if exhausting process of house hunting all over again.

Since we hadn't always been successful at finding a house that suited both heart and pocket, we were very conscious that we had to get it right this time! Jim was still with ATV, so we needed to remain in Hertfordshire and after searching practically the whole county, we came upon the village of Wallington, near the market town of Baldock, right to the north of the county. There we found the most likely house we had seen so far. Nothing is perfect, but we had a good feeling about this one and luckily, in 1976, we managed to buy it.

Three miles from Baldock, Wallington had a pub and a grocer, butcher, baker, milkman and fishmonger who delivered, so we were not in the least cut off. The house had a lot of room and a large garden – and the village was very friendly. The evening we moved in, we found a cauliflower and several necessities kindly left on our doorstep. Help with cleaning the house was easy to find and we settled in happily, staying for nearly twenty years.

That summer there was a terrible heatwave; I think it was the hottest summer ever recorded. The severe drought wasn't good for gardens, but it was excellent for moving in and doing odd jobs outside – I remember cutting carpets to size on the hard, dry, brown lawn. At one point we wondered if the grass would ever recover, but sure enough, in September, the rain came and made it green again.

My mother had her own rooms and when she could no longer go upstairs, she had everything that she needed brought to her spacious downstairs living room. The arrangement worked well for a time, but she had no long-term friends in the village and began to miss her social life. I was very busy with the children, Jim and work and although we took her out and about as much as we could, and entertained people who could provide her with lively company, eventually she decided that she would have a more enjoyable time at Rush Court, the Distressed Gentlefolk's Association Home at Wallingford, near Henley. I'm sure she made the right decision. She had a lot of old friends in the area and a much better social life with people of her own generation than with us.

We visited her regularly and she came to stay at Christmas, until she was too physically frail to do so. Frail she might have been, but her eye for what we were wearing was as keen as ever. We had to be sure we were properly turned out when we went to see her. It was important we were 'up to date' – she wanted her girls to be stylish and was always keen to keep up with what was going on in the fashion world. She never really got ill, apart from breaking her hip after falling down some stairs at a pub in Worthing while she was staying with friends (she saw the funny side as she hadn't even had a drink, only lunch!) – the last of her many accidents – and in the end she just curled up and went to sleep like a serene, peaceful dormouse, at the age of ninety-five.

In the meantime, the children grew up and left home, in theory at least. They still all came back regularly, as children do. Mark was in his shoulder-length hair stage, as of the times, and spent many hours perfecting his guitar playing in his room. He, like Jim, is of a fairly quiet and deep-thinking disposition. Claire, on the other hand, has always been very independent and freedom-loving. Jim was displeased on a regular basis when she got in with a fast crowd and had a much older, car-dealer boyfriend; a powerful, expensive car of one type or another parked in the drive on a number of nights almost drove him crazy, the Jensen Interceptor being one. I kept very quiet, having done exactly the same kind of things myself at her age, and Claire has only discovered this now, from reading and helping me with this book! Rose was really beginning to flourish, since the house move necessitated a change of school. At sixteen years old this change created much worry, but it turned out for the best, because one teacher in particular saw and encouraged the artistic and creative potential in her, which has got her to where she is today. Mark went to Bristol University to study Geology, Claire did a business course at ICI and Rose did a foundation course in Art, later followed by a degree in Theatrical Design at Central St Martin's. Our Labrador, Honey, had to be put to sleep at the age of fourteen and although we acquired another one, a two-year-old that needed a home, she did not settle. She was very disruptive – nothing like our beloved Honey – and we realized she would be far better off somewhere she could run around and use up her boundless energy. So we found her a new home on a farm, where she had a much happier time.

In Baldock, we found a kitten in need of a home, took her in and named her Maud. It is very uncommon to find a ginger queen (female) yet Maud was nearly all ginger, with a tiny white tip to her tail. She loved watching bird and fish programmes on the television. She cemented her place in family lore one day while we were watching a nature documentary, when she got up and went to play near the table, on which was a lightweight red nylon tablecloth. The next thing we knew, she had caught her claw in it and was swirling across the room in front of the television like a matador! We laughed so much!

Maud found a black-and-white husband, or rather he found her, of course, with much caterwauling. Subsequently, she had four kittens in the linen cupboard amongst the piles of towels. It was no use trying to persuade her to go elsewhere, so we just had to let her get on with it. We kept one of the kittens, Edith, a sweet fluffy tortoiseshell ball of fur who grew up to be a ruthless hunter. No small bird or shrew was safe. One morning we watched as a swallow came a little too close to the ground and Edith leapt in the air and batted it down like a tennis player triumphantly smashing the winning ball of a match. She was quite acrobatic when she wanted to be.

Like Honey, Maud died at fourteen. We buried her at

the top of our rockery and poor Edith sat for almost a week, gazing at where she had last seen her. Edith, in her turn, lasted until she was nearly nineteen, leaving the bird population mightily relieved when she finally went.

After dipping my toe in the water with O-level Cookery, I decided to do A-level Art at Hitchin College. Since I had drawn and painted since childhood, it was something I had always wanted to do, but every time I had started an art course in the past, I had been inveigled into modelling instead. Now was my chance to get going. It was really interesting and I managed to do quite well, getting a B grade, which was acceptable, although I had hoped I would do better.

Next, as I was still doing a fair bit of dressmaking to swell the coffers, I thought I would extend my skills in that area too. The City & Guilds course in Fashion sounded just up my street, and manageable too. 'Just one day a week,' they said, omitting to tell me that they actually meant one day at college and the rest of the week doing homework! After the initial shock wore off, I threw myself into it and ended up attending for four years – I got my certificate and made some nice friends along the way, as well as a lot of outfits. We designed and made everything ourselves, which was really challenging.

Our tutors told us to look around and find inspiration in anything that we saw. I took them at their word when

I was making one particular blue two-piece, and drew on the shape of the 'step' roof lines on Dutch houses. I made eight outfits in all, including a cream linen suit, a tailored grey wool 1930s coat and a pink velvet evening dress. The cream suit is not really 'me' any more, but I've still got it. I wore the coat a lot, but it disappeared somewhere along the way. The pink evening dress had to go because I've shrunk as I've got older and it started to swamp me. And the blue two-piece wasn't very good material, so I didn't keep it.

I mostly used cheap fabric – man-made stuff – as I was doing it for the experience and wasn't sure if I would actually want to wear any of the clothes once I'd made them. Hitchin Market then was a wonderful source of material and all the other necessaries. I made a lingerie set – a silk dressing gown and nightdress, which I still have – and a drop-waisted grey 1930s-style dress with a pleated skirt. I very much liked 1930s designs – they had suited my mother so well, and now they suited me, too. My favourite outfit of all was a purple evening dress, which had several flowing folds. I was amazed that I'd created it! It lasted well and I still wear it today.

At least this time there were no foxes to chew up my efforts, just cats to sit on them and put fluff every-where. I continued to make a lot of clothes for myself and other people after I completed the course, mostly special occasion outfits. We still went regularly to Ascot and

Henley and other events throughout the summer season and it was wonderful to know there was virtually no chance of anyone else having the same outfit, as each one I made was completely individual.

I find I don't make so much now, as I have a huge wardrobe. It's more a case of customizing what I already have, ensconced in my sewing room at the top of the house. You don't have to have lived as long as I have to know that fashion has a habit of coming round again. It's always happening – I'm sure I wasn't the only person who noticed that some of the key silhouettes at London Fashion Week 2015 looked very 1950s, with calf-length skirts and small waists. It's uncanny how often I have been about to throw something out, only to see a near-identical garment advertised in the paper as 'the next best thing'.

My travels as Miss Berkertex ended when store modelling was phased out in the 1980s, in favour of advertising in newspapers and magazines, but I went on doing television and film extra work. Over the years I had appeared in *Planemakers*, *General Hospital*, *The Arthur Haynes Show*, *The Benny Hill Show* (no, I wasn't one of his young ladies!), *Within These Walls*, the original *Upstairs, Downstairs*, *Dr Who*, *Shoulder to Shoulder*, *Lovejoy*, several James Bond films (I wasn't a Bond Girl either!) and a lot of costume dramas. I particularly enjoyed the historical programmes, as they took me to many stately homes and

27. *Sunday Times* front cover at seventy-five years old, 6 June 2004.

28. Star attraction at a Procter & Gamble event in Beijing, 2010.

29. *Vogue* China in Dolce & Gabbana, 2010. I loved this suit and wanted to take it home with me.

30. Looking through my portfolio at my agency
Models 1 in 2011.

31. Posing for the *Times Magazine* in September 2012.

32. This photo of me relaxing at home was featured in the *Telegraph* in September 2013.

33. Nancy Honey's portrait of me in my garden for the '100 Leading Ladies of 2014' project.

34. Twinkling in an Alice Temperley dress for *Marie Claire* in China.

35. *Opposite, top*. Wearing a fantastic hat.

36. *Opposite*. This photo was used for the *Drapers* magazine cover in July 2014. I love the blue background.

37. Celebrating my eightieth birthday with my four grandchildren, Alec, Grace, Jack and Robin in London.

38. My grandsons Jack and Alec's eighteenth birthday celebration at Sandhurst.

often provided unique access to rooms that were otherwise out of bounds.

Jim was at ATV at Borehamwood for thirty years in all. As well as *Sunday Night at the London Palladium* he did *Celebrity Squares*, *The Golden Shot*, lots of plays, light entertainment and outside broadcasts, and many popular series. He worked on the live broadcast of Churchill's funeral, the polo at Windsor, presenter and writer Jack Hargreaves's country series, *Out of Town*, *The Worker*, starring the comedian Charlie Drake, and many more. When ATV relinquished Elstree to the BBC, we didn't want to move to the new Nottingham location, so Jim retired from what became Central TV. As he knew the site better than anyone, he agreed to spend three months helping the BBC move into the Elstree site and ended up staying six years as assistant to the head of Elstree, until he officially retired. He then joined the board of the actors' charity, the Royal Theatrical Fund (RTF), and was secretary there until 1997.

Jim loved giving his time to helping people in the acting profession, and their families, who had fallen on hard times. He found it very fulfilling. And he had many friends who worked – or had worked – in the theatre, so it was a cause close to his heart. He always prepared assiduously for the monthly board meetings in which the members would review the cases brought to their attention. They had to make a lot of hard decisions about what level of support the RTF could provide in financial, advisory and other capacities.

Unfortunately, though, Jim's health had been declining for several years. Looking back, the signs had all been there, but no one recognized them, including me. One day, his colleagues at the RTF sent him home from the office in London's Covent Garden, perhaps thinking that his slurred speech and slightly incoherent behaviour was evidence that he was drunk. He came home, rested and felt better enough to carry on as normal – he didn't want any fuss, so there was no trip to the doctor for a check-up and no one realized that he'd had a mild stroke.

A year later he suffered a second, much more serious stroke on the stairs going up to a board meeting at the RTF. He was rushed to University College Hospital on the Euston Road and stayed there for the next three weeks. Although he made a pretty reasonable recovery, he was less able physically now. For me, the most difficult thing was the effect it had on his personality. He became negative and disgruntled, which wasn't like him at all. He could put on a good show for friends and visitors and be charming to them, but the effort took its toll and once they were gone he would revert to being a bad-tempered individual who didn't seem to like it when I was there and liked it even less if I wasn't! It was all rather exhausting – for us both.

*

As a new wife back in 1954 I'd soon realized that if I said to Jim that I'd like to do something and he said no, he didn't think it was a good idea, it was best if I said nothing more about it for a few days. Then he'd say, 'Why don't we do this?' (of course, it would be what I'd previously suggested) and I'd say innocently, 'Oh, yes, I'd love to do that!' Sometimes it just needed time for the idea to crystallize. Thankfully this tactic worked well for the intervening forty-three years!

We decided to move to Baldock, where Jim could have some independence and walk to the shops, station and pub for an enjoyable tipple of whisky and a cigar without needing to drive or be driven. The days of being able to look after a large garden and vegetable patch were behind him. We chose a period townhouse where the large pieces of furniture inherited from my mother wouldn't be out of place. It had a small courtyard garden and was within two minutes' walk of the town's amenities. I really appreciated my work as an extra now, as it got me out of the house and gave me a break from my increasingly demanding role as carer. As long as I got everything ready before I left – the meals prepared and easy to heat up – Jim could manage, even if he grumbled. It was a blessed respite for me to spend time mixing with my friends among the extras and other colleagues on an exciting film or TV production set.

Luckily, I wasn't working and we were at home together when Jim suffered his third, and this time fatal, stroke. It was in April 1997 – he was sitting comfortably in his favourite armchair with the newspaper when he just went kind of funny and fell onto the floor. I called an ambulance, which came very quickly and took him to the Stevenage Lister Hospital, where he died peacefully in his sleep during the early hours of the morning of 27 April, without gaining consciousness. He was seventy-three. Claire and Rose were able to come and sit at his bedside – Rose stayed with me and then Claire took over while Rose took me home for a freshen-up and a rest. Sadly, Mark was in Hong Kong, where he was putting together a book on The Japanese Kodo Drummers, and so he was unable to get there in time, but came as soon as he could. And at Jim's funeral in our beloved church at Wallington, Mark gave a wonderful – and very moving – eulogy.

The shock of Jim's passing was immense. Our life together had been full of such happy memories, as well as some ups and downs, since that first night at the Walter Gore Ballet. When you have shared your life with someone for over forty years, the loss is so great that it feels like your whole life has disappeared. But in some ways it was a tremendous release too. It had been increasingly difficult caring for somebody who was understandably frustrated by the growing limitations caused by their illness.

In the weeks and months that followed, I cried at night and kept myself busy during the day. Like all those who have lost someone dear, I found there was only one way to deal with life and that was to take it a day at a time. Fortunately, I had plenty of commitments for extra work and kept turning up whenever and wherever I was required. Keeping busy and waiting for time to start its healing process most definitely worked for me. I found that, although the sense of sadness and loss doesn't go away, you seem to grow around it and learn to live with it, so that eventually it becomes a part of you, which makes it bearable.

TEN

Dolce & Gabbana Trouser Suit

'Are you sure they want me to do a *catwalk* show?'

My agent had just told me that I had been booked to 'walk' for the designers Red or Dead during London Fashion Week, 1998.

'Quite sure,' my agent said. 'The stylist said you were just what they were looking for.'

It was thrilling news, but I couldn't help feeling apprehensive. Would the clothes fit? Would I fall off the catwalk? It had been more than ten years since my last store modelling job – and nearly fifty years since I had worked regularly as a fashion model. Would I be able to pull it off?

In the event, I was fine. The 1998 Red or Dead fall/ winter collection had a Native American theme, so instead of having to wear much-dreaded high heels, I was able to clump off down the catwalk in a pair of moccasins. I really enjoyed it, especially as I had a handsome male model to accompany me.

Well, that was fun, I thought, expecting it to end there.

A few weeks later, Jo Phillips, the stylist who had 'dis- covered' me for Red or Dead, suggested I contact *Vogue*.

They were doing a feature on ageing and I might be suitable, she said. Wow, I thought, *Vogue*! THE fashion magazine!

Excited, but also slightly daunted, I considered carefully what to wear to the interview. It was important to create the right impression, so I enlisted the help of my designer daughter, Rose, and we went to Fenwick's on Bond Street to buy a new white top and black skirt, a suitably classic outfit for an 'old' model. I felt a bit fluttery as I arrived at Vogue House in Hanover Square, but the people at *Vogue* were not as intimidating as I'd feared. They gave me lots of confidence and I was soon booked for a photo shoot with Nick Knight, one of the world's most famous fashion photographers.

Nick was lovely to work for and made me feel special. The other models were of varying ages: one Russian lady was a hundred and had a very charming smile; the others were between fifty and eighty. It was a very relaxed shoot and the stylist and I had lots of fun trying to find ways for me to wear my figure-hugging Hussein Chalayan dress. It was a beautiful piece of couture design and I loved how it looked when we finally got it right.

Being photographed for *Vogue* was unexpected, but the real surprise of the day was being approached by a very nice woman called Ellis, who was at the shoot scouting for the top London model agency, Models 1.

'I think we would like you on our books,' she said.

'Really? Me?'

A few days later, I presented myself at Models 1 in the King's Road. There I met Jane Wood, the chief booker, a tall, model-like blonde easily young enough to be my daughter. She was probably wondering what Ellis had brought in this time, but she soon put me at ease and sent me off to see James Muldowney, an up-and-coming photographer who would help me update my portfolio, which was seriously in need of an overhaul.

In a Battersea studio with the unforgettable name of the Lemonade Factory, an inventive stylist named Cynthia Lawrence put me in a series of ethereal lace dresses. I'm not sure I felt particularly 'of the moment' as I wafted about the studio looking like Miss Havisham, but the photos were stunning and everyone was very pleased with them.

Before long I was officially on the books of Models 1, as one of their first 'older' models among all the young ones. Life was suddenly extremely busy. It was amazing. There I had been, toddling along doing my extra work, thinking that at least it would keep me off the streets! I'd planned to do some more painting – as well as more walking and more visits to the theatre and galleries – but suddenly there was barely time to pick up a paintbrush.

I couldn't help wondering if it would all end in tears, though. I had heard of other girls who had been picked out like me, only to be dropped after a few assignments.

So I kept up my film and TV extra work until my diary was so packed that my appointments were clashing, at which point I had to make a choice: I decided to concentrate solely on the modelling. At this point the children were living their own individual lives – Mark was expanding his knowledge and creativity with an Art degree, and Claire and Rose were busily occupied with their young families. They were thrilled that I was having fun and in demand!

I did a lot of catwalk shows in those early years. I don't do so many now, as I've got funny feet and can't wear high heels any more, but I've always enjoyed them. Whether it's for *Brides* or Diesel, D&G or DKNY, catwalk shows are madness – always hectic, never on time – and the air buzzes with feverish excitement. You wonder how they create order out of the backstage chaos, but somehow they always manage.

At one show, Vidal Sassoon came up to me and said, 'I wish you'd teach the other models how to walk!' He seemed to like the fact that I don't do anything silly – I just walk normally, without affectation. I find it a job not to smile, though. I always think it's a shame that models look so miserable on the catwalk. I'm not suggesting that anyone should grin like a Cheshire cat, but at Gaby Young's agency we were taught to look pleasant, at the very least.

But I wasn't just doing the catwalk. From the beginning of 1998 I did a lot of different kinds of modelling – for magazine shoots and commercials, too. My first trip abroad with Models 1 was to Marrakech for an Olay commercial in May 1999. I was cast for my ability to do yoga, which I had picked up in the 1950s from Gilbert Adams and his friends down in St Ives. I did several commercials for skincare brands wearing a leotard and holding various yoga poses. Apart from the obvious health benefits, it made me rather glad that I'd kept it up for all those years. I still do my stretches most mornings.

A few weeks after the trip to Marrakech, I flew to Havana to do an advertisement for SWICA health insurance. I did another insurance commercial in Antwerp, this time for AXA, where I appeared in a scene in which I was supposed to have thrown my boyfriend out, and all his belongings too. I had great fun hurling lamps, books, a TV and a radio out of a first-floor flat window at night! In the months and years that followed, I went to Cape Town a few times for Olay, Evian Water and others, and to Skagen in Denmark for Nivea. It wasn't quite international jet-setting, but I was flying business class, earning good money and, more importantly, enjoying myself. After a tough few years and the deep sadness of losing my husband, I felt incredibly fortunate to be busy and working.

One of the best things about modelling is all the people you meet – and they're never strangers for long.

You can't move without meeting people you know when you get to my age. When I went to Stockholm to do an H&M campaign in early 2015, it wasn't long into the shoot before I discovered that the other model had a sister who lived in the same town as me. As it happened, I also knew the photographer, although I'd never worked for her until then.

Quite soon after I joined Models 1, I started being approached by newspapers and magazines to do interviews about my life and career as a model. I've never had a problem doing publicity. It's really easy to talk about yourself! I've also given quite a few talks on the subject of modelling. Fortunately, I've been to enough lectures to know what *not* to do – in other words, how important it is to speak up properly and be clear. At school we were often called upon to talk for two minutes in front of the class about something, which was good training, and I've had a lot of practice reading the lesson in echoey churches. When I first started reading in church, I used to ask Jim to sit at the back and tell me if he could hear me properly – being a stage manager, he was the perfect person to consult on such things.

In 2001 I went to Paris for a week to play a model in an episode of *Absolutely Fabulous* – the one where Patsy and Edina go to Paris for a magazine shoot. It was a lot of fun, especially as I spent most of my time walking on the Pont Alexandre III and around the Café de Flore in the 6th arrondissement. As we 'rested' between set-ups, I drank delicious citron pressé and watched the chic Parisiennes go by – including Sonia Rykiel, the fashion designer, who came into the cafe carrying one of her famous black handbags with silver studs all over it.

We had to wait all day to do our shot, which is par for the course when filming. So it was a lovely surprise to find a present for myself and the other 'model' on our make-up table the next morning – a tiny jug from the Café de Flore with a note from our director, Jennifer Saunders, saying, 'Sorry you were kept so long yesterday.' At our last supper of the shoot in a Chinese restaurant called Dave, Jennifer got a plate with Dave on it from the waiter to give to Dave Gorman, who was playing our photographer in the episode. It was so thoughtful of her – and not something that happens all that often.

The following year I appeared in one of several pop promos I have done – this was the Will Young video for his single 'Light My Fire'. I featured in a family party set-up, wearing a strapless, full-skirted dress with my hair in a chignon, and I had to hold his face affectionately. I remember sitting on a grass bank with him between takes, discussing the merits of learning to dance. He was wondering whether he should, for the future, and of course I encouraged him. I imagine it came quite naturally to him when he did start learning, because he was very accomplished by the time he appeared in *Mrs Henderson Presents* and *Cabaret*.

I also did an advertising shoot for Bupa, in which I was required to wear a swimsuit and stand up to my waist in water, holding a naked baby. All well and good, but we arrived at the swimming pool in Kew one early morning to find that the swimming pool heating had broken down. The director looked at me in dismay. 'Let's just get on with it,' I said, and so we did.

They used twin babies, interchanging them every so often – and I kept warm by holding them close! I was freezing by the time we finished, but a very long, very hot shower soon put me right. The director even took the trouble to ring me the following day to check I was OK!

The whirlwind continued, until I wondered if things were ever going to slow down. I assumed the modelling work would dry up when I got to eighty – surely it had to! – but, to my amazement, I was still going strong up to and beyond my eightieth birthday. By then, I had worked for several of the biggest fashion photographers and magazines in the world and worn clothes by all the major couture houses – Mario Testino, Nick Knight, David Bailey, *Vogue*, *Harpers & Queen*, *Tatler*, Chanel, Dior, Prada. The list went on. I had also worn some incredible jewels and, although I'm a great fan of costume jewellery, I couldn't help being impressed. In 2007 I did a shoot for *Intelligent Life*, the *Economist*'s cultural supplement, for Mary McCartney with fabulous jewellery by Graaf, Tiffany, Asprey and Boucheron, wearing amazing Chanel couture and Asprey frocks – how surprising: I didn't have any idea that Asprey made frocks as well as their famous jewellery! The security was incredible – everything was set out on tables, each with its own guard. You weren't even allowed to go to the loo wearing any of the jewels.

By 2010, aged eighty-two, I was deemed to be 'Britain's oldest working model', which made me sound rather like some contraption that Uncle Heath Robinson might have dreamt up. (And when I was eighty-five I got into the *Guinness Book of Records*.) Imagine how much my twenty-year-old self would have laughed if anyone had suggested that I would still be strutting my stuff well into my eighties!

That year turned out to be one of my busiest: I was sent to Berlin, Prague, Ibiza, Paris and Beijing, and other places too. The year began with a fashion show for my talented young French designer friend Fanny Karst, at the Lycée Français in South Kensington. Fanny designs beautiful and unusual clothes for older women and I'd met her when I modelled for her final degree show at Central St Martin's, now part of the University of the Arts in London. The following day I did a presentation for Jo Sykes at the St Martin's Lane Hotel as part of London Fashion Week. Jo was making tailored and very wearable designs with a quirky twist – later in the year she was snapped up by Aquascutum and became an important member of their in-house design team.

Next I was whisked off to Berlin to be part of the campaign for Wunderkind, whose clothes I love. Suddenly there were pictures of me in all the glossy magazines and shops, wearing stripes and swirls and fringes and chains, with a terrifically handsome, extremely young man by my side. His name was Marco-Alexander and the director had approached him after spotting him in a local Berlin restaurant, where he was having dinner with his parents!

Being different – about fifty years older than your average model – led to me taking part in new creative projects. I was honoured to be among the nine models selected by the renowned photographer Rankin to feature in an exhibition that would be staged at the start of the following year's London Fashion Week. The photographs were a commission for All Walks Beyond the Catwalk, an initiative founded in 2009 by the influential fashion figures Erin O'Connor, Caryn Franklin and Debra Bourne, to promote more diversity in the industry – plus size, each and every race, unusual and older models, no exclusions! I was so pleased to be a part of it, not least because I always enjoy working with Rankin. He's so funny.

A few days later, a job for *She* magazine took me to a stunning Elizabethan manor house in Kent, with fantastic views across the South Downs National Park. Even better, it was for the Christmas issue and the director told us to create a party atmosphere for the photographs. There were lots of models and none of us knew each other, but we pretended to be old friends – and by the end of the day we were all getting on famously.

The following week, at a casting for an American Hotels commercial, I was asked to dance a little – an easy task for me after years of training. As Sinatra's uplifting tones filled the air, I had a blissful time twirling around the studio. The minutes went by and I went on dancing – spinning, swaying, making it up as I went along. After a while I started to think, I'm having a lovely time, but haven't they seen enough?

'Why so long?' I asked the director, when I was eventually asked to stop.

'I was enjoying watching you dance!' she said.

Well, I got the job. To my delight, the shoot was in Prague, somewhere I had never been and had always wanted to go. Luckily, my first day of fittings gave me a free evening, so I set off with a hotel map to see the Charles Bridge, the Astronomical Clock and Wenceslas Square. The next day my call wasn't until one, so I spent the morning exploring the Alphonse Mucha museum.

Then it was time to get down to work. On the half-landing of a beautiful hotel staircase, I was told to start smoochy dancing with a handsome young man –

yes, another one, I'm so lucky! – while a pack of white German shepherd puppies bounded past us. Needless to say, it required quite some effort – and much rattling of food bowls – to persuade the puppies to go up the stairs, and so there were several takes and hours of intermittent smoochy dancing before we were finally let go at midnight. I did not stay on to see the rest of the scenes, but in the finished advert there were kittens, ducklings, more puppies and a deer! It seemed an extraordinary way to advertise hotels, but there was something rather charming about it.

One thing leads to another and I was thrilled when the Wunderkind people recommended me for an advertisement for Mykita spectacles in Ibiza in September. My grandchildren were very amused at the thought of Granny hanging out in the club capital of Europe, but thankfully we stayed at a wonderful family-run hotel without a nightclub in sight or, more importantly, within earshot. We were so far off the beaten track that the signpost to the hotel was written in felt-tip pen.

The days that followed felt just like a holiday, as myself and three other models posed all over the island, wherever the photographer Mark Borthwick needed us. I wore just one outfit, a gorgeous white dress, along with the spectacles, of course – and it was so warm that I only needed a cardigan in the late evening. We had lunch in the beach bars, lay on the sand and ate twilight suppers on our hotel terrace. You could hardly call it work at all. I thoroughly enjoyed myself.

What next? It had not escaped my notice that for several weeks my agent, Elaine – my Models 1 booker since my rediscovery – had been muttering about a job in China. However, with modelling – as with so many things – you don't take a job seriously until you are actually doing it. Yes, you could end up going to China, Russia, Brazil or (with a last-minute change and budget down-grade) Eastbourne – or you could simply spend the week at home twiddling your thumbs. Developing a thick skin has been crucial to my career and sense of self, because disappointment comes with the territory. So many castings and auditions go nowhere. So many jobs don't materialize. It's something I take in my stride. Something I've learned throughout my life, from my early days with horses and from modelling in my twenties, is that it is a fact of life that things don't always go how you'd like or want them to. But it really doesn't matter – in fact, it's fine, because it toughens you up – and there is absolutely no point in worrying about things you have no control over.

But now, all of a sudden, I was being asked to produce my passport in order to get a visa to go to Beijing. My ears pricked up. What was Elaine saying? A shoot for Chinese *Vogue*? A fashion show at a big Procter & Gamble dinner in the Shangri-La Hotel? What an amazing opportunity! I started to take her seriously.

'I'm coming too,' she said. 'You need a nanny!'

'How long is the flight?'

'Nine hours, non-stop.' Pause. 'Business Class.'

At the end of November I set off to Heathrow in my faithful local taxi, wondering what China would be like. Fortunately for us, we were given five-star treatment from the moment we landed, thanks to Santana from the Webber Shandwick Agency. He looked after us from start to finish – he even arranged one of the airport staff to meet us off the aircraft and take our suitcases through customs. We were under his care from thereon in: our journeys smoothed, trips organized and everything paid for. He was such a caring person that we wanted to take him home with us.

Our hotel had eighty floors and magnificent views over Beijing. The cityscape was like something out of a science-fiction film. So many of the buildings looked like an architect's fantasy – they were such strange, unconventional shapes – and the skyline was full of surprises! Our rooms were on the sixty-fourth floor and the lifts were so smooth that you hardly noticed how fast they moved, except for a bit of ear popping. We arrived in the late morning, had lunch and then spent the afternoon in my room trying out various looks for the fashion show with the style and beauty team. Some of the clothes were not suitable after all, as often happens at this stage. Eventually, we settled on an outfit by a Chinese designer,

Lu – a pale grey draped top with black tights and my black shoes.

I had an early night, because I was rehearsing for the show the next day – or so I thought. But things change minute by minute in the fashion world and at nine the next morning I instead found myself in a huge black limousine with Elaine and Santana, driving through the city towards the Great Wall of China. Elaine and I couldn't stop marvelling at the extraordinary buildings and huge motorways; Santana, who had come from Arizona to study Mandarin several years earlier, had seen it all before but was enjoying our wonderstruck expressions.

Santana got our tickets and we walked some of the way along the steep and rugged pathway between the ancient towers that punctuate the Great Wall. Next, we explored the Summer Palace and had lunch at an exclusive restaurant inside the grounds. The day was a whirlwind of sightseeing, but the images that stick in my mind are of a man writing a message on the ground with two hands at once, another man flying a beautiful kite, the Marco Polo Bridge with its rows of stone lions, the hundreds of tuk-tuks in the streets and the public telephones, which looked like a cross between salon hairdryers and great orange insects.

Later, we went to the most fabulous restaurant for dinner. Santana insisted that we have Peking duck and it really was delicious, served and carved in front of us.

My first-course soup arrived in a pumpkin with a fluted edge and the lid leaning on one side. The trouble it must have taken! The fruit salad was similarly sculpted and I hardly dared touch it, it looked so perfectly arranged and sliced.

The following day we shot the *Vogue* photographs in a mini studio next to the hotel restaurant, on the eightieth floor. I wore a gorgeous black trouser suit with a white silk blouse by Dolce & Gabbana – I love D&G clothes, they're always beautifully cut and finished. About eight years before this I had been part of a D&G campaign shot in Milan, and then another in 2007 at Wycombe Park, so I'd had quite enough experience of their outfits to count myself a true fan. I wouldn't normally wear a really smart trouser suit, though. We all wore them in the 1970s, but I tend to wear trousers more casually these days. For smart, I'm much more likely to be in a dress.

Next, I put on a long red gown by Celine, followed by a beautiful green dress by Fendi, all adorned with fabulous Bulgari jewellery. I've never lost my love of dressing-up and I never tire of trying on beautiful clothes. When the shoot was done, it was lunch in the restaurant next door and then on to the rehearsals for the fashion show in the enormous ballroom. Everywhere you looked, there were models accompanied by make-up people and hairdressers, two of whom I recognized from previous shoots – Sam McKnight, who had done my hair for that first British *Vogue* shoot twelve years earlier, and Pat McGrath, the make-up artist. There was much exclaiming and hugging!

The show took place on a huge catwalk in the ball-room, which was packed with people in evening dress sitting at elegantly adorned tables. I was last on, preceded by a video of some of my work, and the applause was amazing. I felt terribly special. When it was all over, a quiz was held on stage and several of us were asked to write something to put in a time capsule to be opened in the future. I wrote that I hoped one day to return to this beautiful city. And still it wasn't time for bed, because after this I was besieged by journalists and cameramen and did several interviews for news programmes and magazines. Eventually, Elaine bravely fended them off and I managed to slip away at one in the morning. The next day, we flew home!

As Elaine and I arrived back at Heathrow, we turned to each other and said, 'Did we just dream that amazing trip?'

You'd think I would have managed a few days off after that but there was no rest for me – I took the Euro-star to Paris the following day for a shoot for the Italian magazine *Gioia*. I was very thankful that I did not have jet lag, because this trip definitely brought me down to earth after the heady heights of Beijing. Arriving in Paris in the evening, I was dismayed to find that my hotel near the Place de la République had no restaurant – it was bed and breakfast only. The staff kindly informed me that there were plenty of places to eat nearby and I quickly found a little place for a quick snack. So there was no chance of letting the China trip go to my head. If ever I'd needed a reminder to keep things in perspective, this was certainly it.

The next morning I was collected and taken to a very modern and wonderful apartment overlooking the Eiffel Tower. I had been on the go for days, but I wasn't in the least daunted by the prospect of the day's schedule – ten outfit changes and an interview with a *Gioia* journalist. I know that some of my friends would be truly appalled by the idea of getting in and out of ten sets of clothes within the space of a few hours, but it's my job and I enjoy it. Recently, I did sixteen complete changes for a shoot, but it was quite manageable. There's always a stylist on hand to help.

The clothes for the *Gioia* shoot were all by well-known designers and it was fun trying them all, though I was not sure about cream-coloured shorts with black tights on an eighty-two-year-old! One lovely red outfit made of Lycra was so tight I could hardly move, but it did look incredible. The skirts were all super short, but I was used to wearing short skirts, as hems seemed to be rising with every passing year. Another suit was trimmed with gold thimbles and pearls – it looked most unusual, but would not have been comfortable for sitting down in! I had fun with a black toreador's hat, and the photographer, Ilaria Orsini, was *sympathique* – I felt that we understood one another, which isn't always the case. Some photographers are better at putting their models at ease than others. To be a really good photographer, you need to be a really good psychologist, with an ability to read each individual model and make him or her feel like they are the most important person in the world. Only then can you bring out the best in them!

The apartment we were shooting in was a minimalist masterpiece and I couldn't help asking the owner where she put things. It turned out that the room dividers opened into sections to reveal all the usual books, papers and paraphernalia of life. An interesting African carving hanging on the wall caught my eye – I was surprised to discover that it was actually a cupboard door.

The assistant went to the nearest shop and brought back a selection of delicious quiches and salads for lunch and the day went very quickly. When I got back to my hotel quite late, I had eaten so much that I didn't need to go out foraging for supper, so the lack of a restaurant wasn't a problem. I had an early night and was ready to go home next morning.

It had been a very busy year and I certainly did not expect to do any more work before Christmas. Then one last job came up, this time for *Volt* magazine. I had never heard of *Volt* but the shoot was taking place on 20 December in a studio in North London, a short taxi ride from King's Cross, so it was an easy journey, if not a very convenient date – and I never like to turn work down if I can help it.

I arrived at the studio to find that the stylist was the engaging Cynthia Lawrence, with whom I had done my very first experimental shoot at the Lemonade Factory twelve years earlier. I also knew the make-up girl, so I instantly felt at home. I had not met the photographer, Andreas Bleckmann, but he was easy to work for and took hundreds of pictures. There were other people being photographed as well so it was a very social time. I spent most of the day leaping around in an Adidas maxi dress that I really liked and would have happily worn home. If only the clothes didn't always have to go back! And who knew that Adidas make dresses as well as sports gear? I certainly didn't!

Still, at least I can keep the make-up on if I like it. They always want to take it off before I go home, but I say, 'No, thank you very much, I'm nicely made up now, I'll keep it on and go on my way.'

I spent that Christmas with my family, who are always very supportive and love hearing stories of my escapades and seeing my photographs. Looking back on 2010, I couldn't help feeling amazed at all the exciting things I'd done and the far-flung places I had been to.

It had been one of my best years for work since I had started modelling again in 1998.

I spent New Year's Eve with friends. 'Any plans for 2011?' one of them asked me as we toasted the coming year.

'I have absolutely no idea what the new year will bring,' I said with a laugh, 'though I am hoping there might be time to do some more painting!'

But, of course, there wasn't.

ELEVEN

A Coned Corset

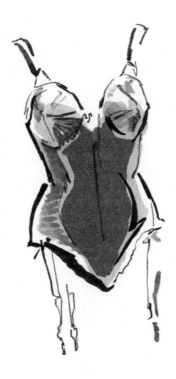

People always seem to marvel at my age, but I'm having so much fun, why would I stop working? I'm just glad that the jobs still keep coming. I don't work quite as often as I did when I first joined Models 1, but the projects are more interesting and often better paid, so I'm happy. My agent has rung me with lots of fabulous assignments over the last few years, and I'm always bumping into old friends – and making new ones – along the way.

Although I am in my mid eighties now, part of me is still very much the girl who used to play dressing-up games on the lawn of our house in Weston-super-Mare. So when I had to wear some very beautiful and expensive clothes for a *Dazed & Confused* magazine shoot in early 2011, I had a lovely time: Chanel, Biba, Prada, Paul Smith, Marc Jacobs, Missoni and Longchamp – you name it, I wore it. Robbie Spencer, the stylist, mixed up vintage and modern designer clothes, and the resulting photos by Ben Toms were widely applauded when they came out. Each fashion story in this particular issue was inspired by a cult film, and Ben had chosen the 1971 film *Harold and Maude*, a love story between a young man and a much older woman. It meant I was again paired with a handsome young model – no complaints from me! – and this time it was Sascha Bailey, David Bailey's son.

The shoot took place at a derelict house just outside Guildford on the Greensand Ridge by the North Downs, a beautiful countryside location. Before we arrived, the owner had been understandably dismayed to discover that all the flagstones on the patio had been stolen in the night. Admittedly the house was due for a makeover, but it was a terrible shock and she was worried that the thieves might return – so, as a deterrent to any further incidents, she asked a friend with a camper van to stay in the grounds. By the time we got there, he had a most welcome bonfire blazing away outside. It was a chilly winter's day and we were glad to sit and drink cups of tea between set-ups.

The photographer had been hoping to shoot at the site for some time and was keen for us to pose by a derelict greenhouse and next to an old car that had been buried by a collapsed garage. Later we went up to the perfect little church of St Martha on the Hill, only accessible by foot, where there were more wonderful views over the countryside of the Surrey Hills.

I love going to all the different locations that my work takes me to, even if I don't get to stay very long. If it hadn't been for my work, I would never have known about St Martha on the Hill; or the dilapidated mansion in Great Tew in the Cotswolds that I visited for my next job, which I was fascinated to learn had once belonged to Viscount Falkland, Secretary of State to Charles I. On my way to the hotel in Moreton-in-Marsh, I suddenly thought of an old friend of mine, Jane Treays. She had been the director of *This Model Life*, a documentary series about models that I had appeared in nearly ten years earlier. Didn't she live nearby? Luckily, when I rang she was free and came to meet me for lunch, so we had a good catch-up!

Along with several other models, I had been booked to do a shoot for the clothing company Toast, who make such chic, wearable clothes. I was looking forward to it, because I would again be working with another old friend, the photographer Sarah Maingot. Sarah and I had done a shoot for Marks & Spencer in Los Angeles a decade before this and we'd had a really fun time, with lots of giggling. Needless to say, we instantly picked up where we had left off and started giggling all over again.

On the morning of the shoot, the crew came to pick me up from my hotel in a magnificent gleaming silver 1970s American Airstream motorhome, which had all mod cons and polished wood fittings. The only disadvantage was that it did nine miles to the gallon and the journey from London had apparently taken hours, as they had to keep stopping for petrol.

We were soon zooming along to Great Tew, a village

so perfectly English – with thatched cottages, neat hedges, a tiny school and an air of old times – that it might have come straight out of Disneyland. We set up our make-up and dressing room in the high attic room of the local pub and headed off to the great house to recce for suitable backgrounds. It was a really special, ancient building, with lots of beautiful rooms and architectural features, now neglected. I felt fortunate to have the chance to explore it. In the grounds, I admired the incredible King Stone, said to have escaped from the circle of stones at Great Rollright, which, legend has it, are impossible to count. Every time you try, you come up with a different number – it's uncanny.

I often travel for work, but I've also done several shoots at home, including an interesting portrait for a photographer friend, Alistair Guy. It was one in a series where he photographed fashion people 'on his knees' – which became the title of the subsequent exhibition – and he chose to portray me in my sewing room at the top of my house, where I have made so many clothes. Alistair is one of my favourite photographers: his work is brilliant and he's very easy to work with. For this particular project, he also photographed Erin O'Connor, Yasmin Sewell and Lulu Guinness, so I felt in very good company.

I saw him again when he invited me to model for a masterclass in photography at the National Portrait Gallery, where he was tutoring fifteen students on the theme of Hollywood glamour and how to achieve it, an event that was linked to an exhibition being held at the gallery. I wore a 1950s-style white shirt and a leopard-print turban, which I felt captured the era very well. I was interested to see how each of the students approached the challenges of lighting and posing the models. Afterwards I looked round the exhibition, which had wonderful portraits of Elizabeth Taylor, Jayne Mansfield and Marilyn Monroe.

At home again, Claire and I posed for a portrait by Julia Fullerton-Batten in a series entitled 'Mothers and Daughters'. Julia brought a crew of nine with her, but I didn't bat an eyelid as I'm used to big shoots and all the related clobber and mess. My furniture had a whizz round the room and the spiders had a big shock, but all was put back and hoovered, so you wouldn't have known they had been. Meanwhile, we did our make-up in the conservatory and made lots of tea.

When it came to the portrait, Claire had to pretend she was leaving after a visit to me – she had to look back at me with a concerned expression, while I sat in my lonely chair, obviously sorry to see her go. It was fascinating to observe Julia's attention to detail. She took infinite pains to get the effects she wanted, which included having a family portrait reflected in the glass table top.

We only met with one problem all day – and that was when she wanted a shot looking in from outside my double doors, which open onto the street. Fine, except that there were cars parked along the kerb and not enough room for the camera. Undaunted, four of the crew lifted the nearest car up bodily and set it down a bit further up the road, out of the way. When they had done the shot, they put it back again! Nothing was going to stand in the way of the picture.

Soon after this, I was off to Dublin to do a shoot for the upmarket fashion store Brown Thomas. This was a very enjoyable trip, not least because of the beautiful designer clothes I got to try on and the incredible steak I sampled at Brooks Hotel. Once again, I was paired with a young man during the shoot for the *Irish Sunday Times*. I was surprised, because I had been expecting to be posing with the older male model – I always seem to get the toyboy nowadays!

Next I did a presentation in one of the elegant upstairs rooms at Somerset House for Geoffrey Finch's Antipodium, which was part of London Fashion Week, wearing a narrow lace skirt, a large white shirt and a pair of men's brogues. It was a very unusual look, but I was just glad not to be wearing high heels! There was a range of models of different ages and we all had our hair straightened and brushed to one side. I rather liked the diamanté nails we were given, too. But it was the hair and make-up team that really caught my eye. A shock of pink hair, a slashed black skirt over striped leggings, crazy make-up and nail art designs – and this wasn't on me or any of the other models! It is always such a joy to be around creative people.

At the end of 2011, I went back to Paris to do another show for Fanny Karst, whose designs for older folk are always elegant and comfortable, but with a certain quirkiness that I adore. I was nicely 'nannied' on the trip by Fanny's cousin, Sophie, who lives in London. When I arrived at the Gare du Nord, she met me from the train and guided me round the Metro until we popped up at a cafe near the venue, where we had lunch sitting outside in the sun with Fanny and her family. *C'est la vie!*

Fanny put on her show with Jehanne de Wavrechin at the Trinquet de Cavalerie, a fencing gym with a huge bare studio that Fanny's family magically transformed into a smart catwalk venue, adding flowers, tables and chairs, and screens at one end for the models to change behind. I always look forward to Fanny's shows because I can rely on the fact that the shoes will be comfy. This time it was Prada platform lace-ups, just the thing to feel absolutely safe in, and very stylish too. There were some nice write-ups in both English and French magazines afterwards.

The year wound up with one last shoot in a studio in Hackney for *Schön!* magazine. The article was called 'Beauty Pageant' and featured myself and three other older models – Paula Hamilton, Jan de Villeneuve and

Tania Mallet. To my delight, we were to be dressed in very glamorous furs, jewels and tiaras. It was so wonderful to be able to wear clothes that would be wholly unsuitable for my normal life.

After a difficult journey hampered by bus diversions to avoid protesting students, I arrived just in time and made a beeline for the rail of outfits that the stylist had put out. There, on a hanger, I saw the most gorgeous coat in the entire world. It was a Michael Kors design and it was pink and furry – the most deliciously comfy coat I have ever worn. I really hoped I would get to wear it for the shoot, and I got my wish! I would quite happily have kept it on for several days.

I love unusual clothes and I'm pretty much game for anything, so I've done some very weird photographs. In fact, I seem to attract them. I did a really interesting project in 2009 with the fashion photographer Marko Dutka, where I was portrayed as self-portraits of Old Master artists, including Dürer, Turner, Reynolds and Rembrandt – all men! – and the photographer and stylist recreated these paintings using me, an older woman. The aim of the project was to start a discussion by evoking the spirit of these historic paintings. Great costumes and hair – I really enjoyed it, and the exhibition attracted considerable attention as it toured around the world.

Only occasionally do I wonder whether I have bitten off more than I can chew. In January 2012, Oxfam approached my agent to ask if I would be interested in taking part in their Big Bra Hunt campaign to get people to donate their bras for women in developing countries. That's how I ended up in newspapers and posters all over the country wearing a replica of the bra and corset that Jean Paul Gaultier designed for Madonna's Blond Ambition tour in 1990.

Everyone was very complimentary about the pictures by Perou, the photographer, and the publicity I did seemed to reverberate around the world. I even had a fan letter from a woman in Phoenix, Arizona. It was a very worthwhile project and we were all happy to give our services, but I must admit that, at one point during the shoot, I thought: *What am I doing being photographed in a corset? I'M EIGHTY-THREE!*

I calmed myself down by thinking back to the 1950s, when it was normal to wear corsets and everybody had them. Somehow that was a comfort.

I would never want to stop experimenting, though. I've got a young photographer friend called Rosie Collins and she's wild. She came and did a shoot in my home just after the Olympics finished in 2012. She had me riding my exercise bicycle on the lawn in a fabulous dress with my slippers on, doing Mo Farah's 'Mobot' pose.

Next, she wanted to photograph me doing something in – or perhaps out of – an aeroplane. But my agent, Chantal, said no.

'I don't mind,' I said. 'I've been in lots of aeroplanes, although admittedly I haven't jumped out of one yet.'

'No, no, we can't manage the insurance!' Chantal insisted.

'Does it make a difference that my daughter Claire is a record-holding skydiver?' I went on. 'It probably runs in the family.'

'No,' Chantal said firmly.

So Rosie decided that she wanted to photograph me dressed as a circus ringmaster, cracking a whip.

Well, I thought, why not? Another fun shoot to look forward to!

It helps being able to wear clothes with confidence. My friends always say that I'd look nice in a bin bag and a couple of years ago I was able to put this to the test. I was asked to pose as Batman's granny at a very strange exhibition at The Gallery in Redchurch Street, in Shoreditch, East London – and of course agreed. The French photographer Gérard Rancinan suddenly hit on the idea of shooting a pietà, me being the Madonna and the young man – Philip Alexander, a dancer – as the dead Christ lying on my lap.

'But we haven't got a dress,' he said.

So the designer cut up two black bin bags and made me a dress, there and then.

And you know what? It didn't look bad at all.

Life is much more fun if you are adaptable and don't

mind what you do. I also think that you have a much more pleasant time if you're tolerant. If someone bumps against me on the London Underground, I usually smile or laugh. I don't get upset about it. It is essential when you are a model not to take things personally. If you don't get a job, it's not your fault. It's all about what *they* want, so get over it. On to the next! That's my attitude.

However, it is wonderful when you *do* get the job and I was thrilled when my agent rang to say I had been booked to do another Dolce & Gabbana campaign. Working for D&G is very prestigious, even though they always do group shots rather than photographing the models individually. It would be a nice trip to Milan, I thought, and I very much like the designers. There is never any fuss or prima donna feeling with them, even though they are so well known.

Two days later, I learned that I was to fly out on a Sunday and stay at the Excelsior Palace Hotel, near Catania. I pored over my street map of Milan, but could not find Catania. It must be in the suburbs, I decided.

E-ticket in hand, I sailed through customs at Gatwick airport and headed for the departure gate. Our destination was posted as Catania, which I had to presume was the name of an airport near Milan. On the aeroplane, I was a tiny bit worried when a woman with a very small baby came to take the window seat next to my aisle seat. Would the baby be good on the flight? Then the pilot

The Way We Wore

that rather long for a flight to Milan?

As it turned out, the baby was the sweetest and
quietest child you could imagine. She looked out of the
window, gurgled, jigged up and down and then went to
sleep until we landed. I soon got talking to her mother,
who was going home for a holiday to her husband's family
in Sicily. As we were coming in to land, she looked out of
the window and exclaimed, 'There's Mount Etna!' Finally,
it dawned on me that Catania was in Sicily, and so was I.

I was met at the airport by a taxi that drove me and
another of the crew to the Excelsior Palace Hotel in
Taormina, an hour away. We arrived after dark, had
dinner and went to our rooms, as our call was to be at
seven the next morning. It was dark when we got up
and I couldn't see anything much out of my window.
I could make out some mountains to the right, but the
rest looked like a misty valley. As it got lighter, I realized
I was looking out over the sea, far below the hotel!

We were taken to a nearby hotel, the Metropole,
where everything was set up – food, wardrobe, make-up
and lots more people. There was delicious red blood
orange juice for breakfast, which I remembered having on
the last D&G trip, in Milan. The Metropole also overlooked the sea – everything in Sicily seemed to be on the
side of a mountain or up a stairway. The roads either went
through tunnels or out on gantries winding round the

260

mountains. Every time I got into a car I thought of the children's game Mouse Trap.

The first day of the trip was the shoot for the men's edition, so there were lots of handsome men to work with. The lovely Italian photographer Mariano Vivanco made me feel like a star, even though the men were the focus, and I had some gorgeous clothes to wear – mostly cream and black and very comfortable. We filmed around the square in Taormina, not far from the Metropole, and in the afternoon we posed on a huge flight of steps in the town. It was a fine day and I really enjoyed the beautiful surroundings.

We finished at about six in the evening and went back to our various hotels to change. There was a brief opportunity to look at the shops on the way, but not really time to buy anything, as we were all to meet later and walk to what was said to be the best restaurant in town. It was quite a task to find it, as everyone seemed to have very different ideas as to where it was, but it definitely proved itself worthy of its reputation when we arrived. The proprietor went out of his way to introduce us to a variety of fish dishes and we tried octopus, tuna and grouper, all accompanied by local wine. It was a memorable evening, though not a late one, as we had another seven o'clock start the following morning.

For the womenswear shoot, we were based at the Timeo Hotel, which had been built as a home by Florence

Trevelyan in the nineteenth century. The rooms were all palatial and opened out onto a terrace overlooking the sea and the wonderful gardens she created more than a century before. Behind the hotel I could just see the remains of a Greek theatre, which is still in use. I was told that one night when the opera *Nabucco* was being performed, Mount Etna erupted, providing the most dramatic backdrop!

For this shoot we had a different photographer and crew, and some young female models in place of the men from the day before. The weather wasn't so kind – still fine, but colder – and I don't know whether it was the temperature or the different people, but the shoot was not nearly so relaxed. The clothes were beautiful and very dressy. I loved them, although they wouldn't have been at all suitable for my day-to-day lifestyle. We filmed on the terrace of the hotel and at some interesting locations around the town, but it was chilly in the wind and I was glad to dive indoors at any opportunity because these days I feel the cold very easily. Still, there were a few light-hearted moments. The shopkeepers were lovely and while we were working by the market square, a chap running the candy-floss stall gave us all samples to try, which cheered us up no end.

The next big campaign I did was for TK Maxx, posing in nice wearable designer clothes for their 2013 commercial and winter campaign. This called for a relatively conventional approach to modelling. Then I did a rather striking shoot for *S Moda*, the lovely Spanish fashion magazine, wearing couture leather, lace, sequins, animal prints and big statement jewellery, including a stunning leopard necklace. For the cover I wore Gucci and had my hair styled in a ponytail with large gold hoop earrings. After that I did a really wild shoot for Louie Banks for *Blanc* magazine, wearing some truly extraordinary clothes, many of which were made of rubber. They were certainly nothing like anything I would wear at home, but that's the fun, isn't it? Some of the pieces were made by Franc Fernandez, the designer who did the 'meat' dress for Lady Gaga, and much wriggling was required to get them on and off. The photographer was very young and I kept surprising him with my ability to invent poses to suit the clothes and his ideas. It was a really good day.

This was also the year I appeared in the pop promo for Paul McCartney's single 'Queenie Eye'. He was so nice and I was glad that I could say that I had worked a couple of times for his daughter Mary. Between set-ups I found myself in the green room with James Corden and Johnny Depp. I didn't know James Corden, but was able to say to Johnny Depp, 'I did some filming with you once.'

He was curious to know more, but I couldn't for the life of me remember the name of the film! I described it to him and how we had filmed in front of a blue screen, because it was all CGI, and he was on a horse . . . he remembered the film but could not recall its title either (later I remembered that it was *Sleepy Hollow*!). So we had a good laugh about that and it got the conversation going.

Another highlight of the year was taking part in *Fabulous Fashionistas*, a documentary directed by Sue Bourne. Sue said it was 'exploring the art of ageing in the company of six extraordinary, stylish women. With an average age of eighty, they're all determined to squeeze the pips out of life!' That about summed it up.

I had a lovely time doing the filming and later meeting all the others at a lunch party – Bridget Sojourner was the only one I had met before, whilst modelling with Fanny Karst, so it was really good to also meet Gillian Lynne, the choreographer best known for her work on Andrew Lloyd-Webber's musical *Cats*, Sue Kreitzman, who makes colourful Outsider art, Baroness Trumpington from the House of Lords and Jean Woods from Bath, who's also a big lover of fashion. I found them all very friendly and interesting. Being in the film certainly sparked off more interesting work for me, especially as I was the only professional model amongst them. It was shown on Channel 4 – it has since been screened all over the world and is still going.

I went on to do lots of interviews for UK and Australian radio, Dutch TV, Greek TV and various European magazines, ending the year with a fashion show in Braganza, Italy, for Diesel, at their amazing new factory. It was an in-house show for all the workers and staff. How inspiring it must have been! I was one of forty-six models, forty-five of whom were under twenty-five, many of them sporting incredible tattoos. They were such fun and so kind to me, translating the Italian menu at dinner. There were yet more interviews in 2014 – for Chile, Norway, Brazil and New Zealand. I went to Clarence House as part of my contribution to the Women of the World Festival (WOW), and mentored students at the South Bank. WOW aims to raise and explore the concerns of girls and women here and around the world, while celebrating their potential to make a different and more successful society for everyone.

I did a beauty project at Selfridges for Dove, a shoot for a Colombian magazine and a really lovely cover and inside fashion shoot for *Drapers* magazine. I took part in the Old Trafford Shopping Centre campaign at the extraordinary White House in Ealing, which was not the Arts and Crafts house I was expecting, but a replica Polish mansion. I was then photographed by Nancy Honey for her '100 Leading Ladies' project, which was exhibited at Somerset House in October 2014 and subsequently toured the country. And on it goes. The last job I did at the time of writing was an & Other Stories campaign at H&M's head office in Stockholm, where I had the usual multiple changes of clothing and extremely comfortable Van shoes.

Modelling is such an amazing thing to do, if you're lucky enough to do it. It takes you all over the world, you meet fantastic people, wear gorgeous clothes and actually get paid for it – and you don't have to work every day. All right, you don't necessarily have something to look forward to, because you don't know when you're next going to work, but you always hope there might be something up ahead – and just when you decide they've given you up for good, something turns up.

Thinking back to my early life and those times long gone, I realize that my parents wouldn't recognize my life today. It's the technological advances that would really amaze them. Mobile phones and iPads make life as a model so much easier – texting from a delayed train instead of having to hunt for a telephone box and a threepenny bit, and no more lugging around a heavy A3 portfolio. It's a different world. It may seem quite peculiar to be modelling at eighty-seven years old, but amazing things are happening to people who are even older than me. Take my friend Michael Tibbs. Michael is my school friend Ann's handsome older brother, whom all the girls at Queen Anne's were so keen to meet when he visited his sister at school during the war and, at ninety-three, he has just written a memoir about his naval career in submarines, called *Hello Lad, COME TO JOIN THE NAVY?*, which was published by the Memoir Club in 2013.

You never know what's going to turn up next, even at this age. Life is very surprising and it is not very long, so you might as well get the best out of it. But how do you do that? It helps to be interested in everything. My father gave me the great gift of curiosity and it has never left me. I'm always looking at things. For the last ten years I've been a keen participant in Andrew Davies's All About London and All About Britain walking tours. There's almost nothing I enjoy more than an interesting few hours exploring London on foot. Andrew encourages us to 'look up, down and round the back'. I'm a bit short-sighted, but I look up and all around me wherever I am. That's why I take my seat stick with me on these occasions. I hardly ever sit on it, but it's good for leaning on when I'm looking up and around.

My wardrobe today is an eclectic mix of all the clothes I've kept over my lifetime, including my first shoes, my first wool bathing suit and some of my clothes from the 1940s and 1950s. I have some of my mother's hats and scarves, my mother-in-law's 1920s and 1930s dresses and hats and many unique outfits I've made for myself on my sewing machines – as well as all the 'vintage' clothes and accessories I've picked up along the way in recent years. In winter, I'm always searching for ways to stay warm and still look good; in summer, I love loose dresses and hats. My daughter Rose calls my style 'classy funky'!

I've no idea what the future holds, so it's important to make the most of today. Live in the present, as they say. I've got lots of sayings that I've picked up along the way. 'A smile is as good as a facelift' is a goodie. I also like, 'Growing old is compulsory, growing up is optional.'

Being of a positive nature certainly makes a difference. I've got a friend who looks on the black side of everything. It's quite difficult to go out with her, because you start to wilt in her company after a while. She's gorgeous really and I just love her to bits, but I do wish I could get her to be more positive.

It helps that I've been lucky with my health, too. I've had the odd thing, of course, and I've got funny feet at the moment, something called vasculitis. Don't get it! It's a virus and I'm stuck with it, apparently. Fortunately, I've only got it in my feet, so it could be worse. High heels are out, because it makes my balance a bit strange, but it doesn't stop me getting on with life. Just recently, I went with a friend to Ravensburgh Castle, an Iron Age fort in Hertfordshire. I was expecting a huge great mound of earth – and that's what it was – but I wasn't expecting it to be covered in brambles and rough bushes. The walking was really difficult and afterwards I thought, if I can do that walk, I can do anything.

I'm often asked what my beauty regime is. I'm lucky

to be naturally energetic and slim, but I have always slept well and eaten healthily. My family are quite long-lived so the genes must be good! I eat nearly everything I want, but always in moderation. I drink a lot of water and hardly ever buy ready-made food, preferring to cook my own. Throughout my life, we mostly grew our own vegetables at home, though I do not do that so much now. I have always exercised – horse riding, dancing, cycling and walking – and of course gardening and housework all counts!

I choose the amount of make-up I wear according to the occasion, and always take it off at night. 'Cleanse, tone and nourish' as they say! I love to try new types of make-up and skin care, but never anything very extravagant unless it's given to me as a present, which is always a nice treat. I wash my hair once a week, according to circumstances. As it is quite fine and becoming thinner, I am always trying to find products to combat this. I rarely go to the hairdresser – they always want to cut it off! If it gets too long I trim the end of my ponytail or my daughters will do it for me more efficiently. I don't wear it loose except for work, as it flies about and gets in the way, and at my age I prefer it up anyway. Having it long and able to wear it up is so much easier than having it short, otherwise I'd be endlessly at the hairdresser! I used to tint it when it first showed signs of grey but I got so fed up with having to do it every three weeks that I gave up at the age of sixty, letting it go natural. And what happened? I got more work! As I was doing a lot of extra work at the time, it is apparently more expensive to create a wig (to cover over dyed hair) than to dress one's own! Regarding cosmetic surgery, I have never considered it and wouldn't change my mind – I'm going to age anyway, it's a natural process, so I might as well just accept it rather than fight it. I do see that it can have a positive outcome for some people, so I would never criticize anyone for going down that route in order to feel better about themselves and their lives.

What can one say about today's size 0 models? I have never been a size 0! Some people are naturally thin and fashion loves a thin model! I've never had to go to extreme lengths to be like that – my health is more important to me – though I know people do. I will wear any size as long as it suits me and is comfortable. For work I am usually a size 10, possibly an 8 on some occasions – it depends on the brand of clothing as all sizes seem to vary these days. When I was younger I was five foot seven and a half inches but I'm shrinking, so I'm now five foot six!

I still have a lot of friends, although many of my contemporaries have sadly died. My best friend, Beryl Bateson, died of cancer in 2002. It was a great pity, and I was very sad to lose her, because she was such good fun. She worked at the Opera House for many years, where she was PA to Margot Fonteyn, and then she retired and worked for an optician in Guildford. It wasn't exactly on my doorstep, but we used to meet a lot. I still have Sheila from Queen Anne's School – she lives in Wantage and I often go and stay with her. We have lots of fun attending events together in her neck of the woods – like me, she loves to go out and do things. I've also latched onto some of the girls who were three years below me at school.

Luckily, I've still got a lot of friends from when I was married, many of whom live locally. And, looking back, I realize that many of my friendships have lasted several decades. But a lot of my friends now are considerably younger than me. I migrate towards younger people – and if you have a young outlook, which I fondly imagine that I might have, they quite like you too. I still go to St Ives every year, where I have old friends, and the children of friends have become friends. They all know me down there as the one who modelled for Barbara Hepworth.

Some years ago, I was invited to join the Grand Order of the Lady Ratlings, the women's branch of the Grand Order of the Water Rats, which was set up in 1889. The main objective of this wonderful organization is to foster the spirit of friendship and goodwill towards all – and we host functions to raise money for people who have fallen on hard times. You have to be connected to showbiz to be a member and I got in because of the dancing I did in the 1950s, and my work as an extra. Among the Brother

Rats and Sister Ratlings are both the famous and not so famous, including Punch and Judy men and women, musicians, clowns, comedians, actors, magicians, ventriloquists, jugglers, dancers, singers, agents and rock stars. The Grand Order of the Lady Ratlings is a great, vivacious group of women and since we have a lot of fun working for good causes, I'm very proud and glad to be a member.

I'm close to my children and grandchildren, and proud of them all. Mark, a retired stockbroker, is creative and adventurous by nature. A fine photographer, artist, musician and expeditionist, he lived in Japan for ten years, is currently 'working with words' at a meditation centre in India, and writing a book on tarot reading.

Along with my love of dressing-up, Claire has inherited my adventurous nature and she met her husband, Dick Trigger of the Parachute Regiment, when she was a professional skydiver as a member of the Flying Crusaders demonstration team for the *Daily Express* in 1988, jumping into displays around the UK. She was part of the Women's 100 Way World Record team in 1992. With Dick, who tragically died long before his time in 2000, she has twin sons, Jack and Alec, born in 1993. Claire has loved being a mother to energetic boys and when they were ten years old she took them to live in the South of France, to explore the culture, language, mountains and sea. Wonderfully, they both went up to

Oxford University to study Engineering: Jack is now yacht racing full-time, a passion he has had since he was six; Alec has been rowing for Oriel College and is currently in the Oxford Lightweights Blue boat. And, I'm happy to say, they are both very stylish young men! Meanwhile, Claire has recently qualified as a carpenter and is enjoying building her family a contemporary style eco-passive home with views of rolling countryside in Surrey. When she is not wielding a drill, she is helping me get online at daphneselfe.com.

Rose says that growing up having her grandmother Myra's clothes to play with – and watching me make my own clothes – has given her a love of vintage glamour, fine fabrics and quality workmanship. What is considered fashionable comes second to the personal and often magical stories Rose expresses through her clothes. She first graduated in theatre and costume design and then became a successful couture designer. Today, she is studying for a Master's degree in Fine Art and lives in Dorset.

Her daughter, my granddaughter, Grace, is studying photography, and aiming for a degree in Graphics and Communication. She is gloriously fearless about what she wants to wear, and carries it off with immense confidence. Her brother, my grandson Robin, is at school studying for his GCSEs and training to be a Football Association (FA) coach. He has a very stylish originality combined with a laid-back approach to fashion.

As for what's next for me, I'm currently putting my lifetime of modelling experience into an online modelling course called The Daphne Selfe Academy. I absolutely love working with the next generation of models and other young people. I've so enjoyed my mentoring with WOW, spending time with the students, answering their questions and giving my advice and opinions; and with the online academy, I can reach beyond London and the Home Counties to the rest of the country and even around the world to pass on what I know. There are things I've learned that could be useful to someone just starting out, from how to behave professionally to avoiding the many pitfalls along the way. It will mean learning to get to grips more fully with the Internet and unheard-of things like webinars, but that is today's world and I've never been one to shy away from a challenge! Aside from the academy, the next modelling campaign is coming out any minute and who knows what bookings will come in next week. Will there ever be time for that leisurely painting? Not quite yet, I don't think!

I feel very grateful for the incredible life I have led. With each day that passes, I'm more thankful than ever for my fortunate life and being blessed with a positive and joyful outlook. My Christian faith has always been part of my life and something I have leaned on in tough times. I've seen and learned first-hand – from my parents, my family and others, through the Great Depression, the Second World War and other misfortunes along life's journey – about what is important and how to find happiness in, and appreciation of, each day and circumstance. Life, with all its inevitable ups and downs, is not always easy, but it is a precious gift. To be able to make a contribution daily and inspire others to live fully is the most wonderful reward in itself. And I'm still looking forward to whatever tomorrow brings.

Acknowledgements

When I first started writing my story I intended it just for my family, but over time people kept saying they would like to hear about my life, so I was persuaded to get it into print. It proved quite difficult at first as no one wanted to know until I found the present publishers. I have read so many tales of woe and adversity, though succeeding against all the odds in the end, that I didn't think mine was of much interest. Obviously I have had the normal ups and downs of sadness and loss, but on the whole mine has been a lucky and happy life.

I would like to thank my children Mark, Claire and Rose, my grandchildren Jack, Alec, Grace and Robin, my cousins Monica and Ellie and all my extended family and friends who have encouraged me, but chiefly to my wonderful daughter Claire, whose help and expertise with modern technology has got me through it all. I like to think she is a 'chip off the old block' with her energy and help, but with a more modern and up-to-date outlook!

I would also like to thank everyone involved, especially Rebecca Cripps, Gordon Wise of Curtis Brown, Georgina Morley, Dusty Miller and all the Pan Macmillan team, and of course all the lovely people at my agency Models 1, chiefly Chantal and Uwe, for all their continuing help and support in this exciting project.

Picture Acknowledgements

All photographs from the author's own collection, apart from:

26 © Terry O'Neill / Hulton Archive / Getty Images

27 © John Swannell / Camera Press

28 © ChinaFotoPress / Getty Images

29 © Trunk Xu

30 © Alistair Guy

31 © Brendan Freeman

32 © Anna Huix / Contour by Getty Images

33 © Nancy Honey / Camera Press

34 © Rosie Collins

35 © Rosie Collins

36 © Jeff Hahn, styled by Graeme Moran for *Drapers* magazine